RURAL ENGLAND 1996

Presented to Parliament

by the Secretary of State for the Environment and the

Minister of Agriculture, Fisheries and Food by Command of Her Majesty

October 1996

Cm 3444

£11

DDP Services
Published by the Department of Environment
Printed on recycled paper
October 1996

FOREWORD

The 1995 White Paper *Rural England* set a comprehensive framework for sustainable development in the countryside, unprecedented at least since the Scott Report of 1942. Yet it was not intended to be the last word on our countryside, rather the beginning of a healthy and open debate. And so it has proved. *Rural England* has been read and discussed the length and breadth of the country. This widespread interest and sense of ownership is as it should be, for the English countryside is not the preserve of Government but belongs to us all, wherever we live, and we all share a responsibility for its protection and prosperity. Equally we recognise that protection and prosperity cannot be achieved without the active support of rural communities.

Rural England 1996 reports on the progress that has been made in the 12 months since the publication of the White Paper. During that time we have worked hard to honour the commitments we made. We have wrestled with the challenge posed by our household projections, revised planning guidance for the countryside to reflect the principles and objectives set out in *Rural England*, prepared the ground for legislation which will give greater powers to parish councils and reduce the burden of rates on village shops, and expanded Countryside Stewardship.

Others outside national Government have played an important part too, and *Rural England 1996* reports on some of the initiatives which they have taken in the last twelve months and which may inspire others to follow their example. They include action by local authorities to develop rural strategies and Local Agenda 21 projects, by voluntary organisations and volunteers to help the homeless and to enhance biodiversity, by communities to support their village shop, by farmers and other small businesses to expand and diversify, and by new partnerships to regenerate their locality.

The success of *Rural England* should not be judged on one year alone, nor was its publication an isolated event, but rather the start of a process. We have achieved much in the last year - we in Government together with our many partners across the countryside. Yet there have been set-backs too, most notably the repercussions of BSE for farmers, for other businesses and for the environment, and there remains more to be done if we are to turn *Rural England's* objectives into reality. We need to set sharper targets, to develop more reliable indicators of progress and to continue to identify cost effective measures to achieve them. That is the challenge for future years. This first progress report is a step along the way.

SECRETARY OF STATE FOR THE ENVIRONMENT

MINISTER FOR AGRICULTURE,
FISHERIES AND FOOD

CONTENTS

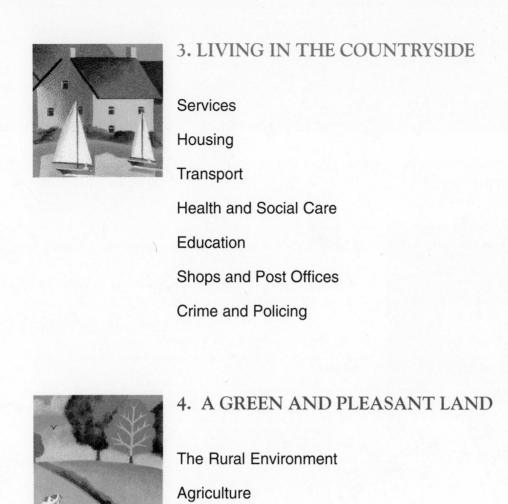

1. GOVERNMENT AND PEOPLE

INTRODUCTION

Rural Development Commission/M Hancock

Reeth Rural Workshop, North Yorkshire

Rural England, which was published in October 1995, was the result of the most comprehensive review of the English countryside ever undertaken by Government. We examined the changes which have taken place in the countryside and set out our vision for its future. *Rural England* was about a living and working countryside. We analysed the practical implications of sustainable development for the jobs, the services and the environment of our countryside and for the people who live and work there.

Principles

Rural England established a strategic framework for our approach to the countryside, based on a set of principles against which to measure our actions. It made clear that:

- the countryside is a national asset. We value it for its own sake, but we must also respect the priorities of those who live there;

- reconciliation of competing priorities requires a willingness on all our parts to appreciate each others' perspectives and dialogue between local communities, local authorities and Government Departments;

- responsibility for the countryside is shared between many partners. Local people are generally best placed to identify their own needs and the solutions to them, so we must involve them in more of the decisions which affect their daily lives, be responsive to their priorities and work in partnership with them;

- policies must reflect the character of the countryside and be sensitive to its economic and social diversity;

- policies should be based on sound science and good information about changing trends.

Objectives

Rural England also committed us to the pursuit of sustainable development, which requires us to manage the countryside in ways that meet current needs without compromising the ability of future generations to meet theirs. This involves:

- meeting the economic and social needs of people who live in rural areas;

- conserving the character of the countryside;

- accommodating necessary change while maintaining and enhancing the quality of the environment for local people and visitors;

- encouraging active communities which take the initiative to solve their problems themselves;

- improving the viability of existing villages and market towns by promoting opportunities for housing and jobs;

- recognising the interdependence of urban and rural policies.

DIALOGUE

Rural England was built on the foundation of widespread consultation - a process which immeasurably strengthened the document and ensured general endorsement of its approach. This debate about the future of our countryside has continued. It has done so with vigour, and we very much welcome the interest and discussion which it has helped to foster.

It is a mark of this interest that the first print run of *Rural England* sold out within two weeks of its launch, and over 7,500 copies have now been sold. We have distributed over 70,000 free copies of the summary document, including one to every parish and town council in England.

A large number of conferences and seminars have been held across the country, and more are planned. Voluntary agencies, parish, district and county councils have been active in arranging discussion. Government Ministers have participated in over fifty such meetings, and officials from Whitehall Departments and Government Offices in many more. **We shall continue to encourage and participate in debate which relates *Rural England's* framework to local circumstances and which leads to a clearer articulation of rural priorities and actions to achieve them.**

The House of Commons Environment Select Committee conducted an enquiry into *Rural England* in the spring of 1996, and its report was published in April[1]. The Committee welcomed the initiative which prompted the analysis of rural life and rural policy and particularly commended the process of consultation and cooperation which contributed to its formation. We published our response in July[2], and we refer separately to some of the Committee's recommendations later in this progress report.

The Environment Select Committee's enquiry emphasised the importance of:

- developing targets as a means of measuring progress and of reporting annually;

- correcting perceptions of a rural idyll by acknowledging the problem of hidden poverty in the countryside;

- sustaining the vitality of market towns;

- wide consultation on how a doubling of woodland could be achieved in ways that optimise economic, social and environmental benefits;

- close working relations between MAFF and the Government Offices for the Region.

[1]*Environment Committee Third Report: Rural England, The Rural White Paper, HMSO*
[2]*Government Response to the Environment Committee Third Report into Rural England, The Rural White Paper, HMSO*

Yorkshire Rural Community Council

Many rural community councils have been active in promoting debate about *Rural England*. The Yorkshire Rural Community Council distributed a "Parish Pack" to local groups, voluntary organisations and all parish councils in the region to help them to discuss the issues raised and to make their own presentations. In co-operation with the Yorkshire Local Councils Association, they also held a series of seven seminars across the county and collated feedback in a report which they presented at a conference on *Rural England* in July 1996. The Community Council also made *Rural England* the theme of its stand at the Great Yorkshire Show in July.

Progress Report

In support of our strategic framework for the countryside, *Rural England* commits the Government to well over a hundred specific actions. It is part of our philosophy that if commitments are made they should be followed through to practical action, and that progress should be monitored and reported. This document therefore reports on our progress in achieving the commitments made in *Rural England* in the year since it was published as well as on new commitments we have made. Specific references to commitments made in *Rural England* are marked by

National Government does not have sole responsibility for shaping and securing the future of the countryside - that is shared amongst us all. Like *Rural England*, therefore, this report describes some of the actions taken by people outside national Government since October 1995 - for example by local authorities, voluntary organisations and businesses. These actions may not have been taken because of *Rural England*, but they share the objectives set by it and help us all to achieve them.

In order to maintain the momentum initiated by *Rural England* we will report on progress annually. Reports will continue to be produced jointly by the Department of the Environment (DOE) and the Ministry of Agriculture, Fisheries and Food (MAFF) in close cooperation with others.

Targets and Indicators

Targets can help to give a sharper sense of direction to policies and to their implementation and development. In preparing annual reports therefore we shall look for opportunities to set quantifiable targets and report on progress towards achieving them. The targets which we identify will be based on an understanding of the sorts of measures likely to be needed to achieve them. These targets may be firm and binding. They may also be "indicative" where the goals are longer term or where the action necessary to achieve them requires the cooperation of partners beyond national Government.

Some Government targets which relate to our rural objectives include:

- ensuring that half of all new housing is built on re-used sites by 2005;

- aiming to reduce the proportion of homes lying empty to 3% by 2005;

- seeking a doubling of woodland in England over the next half century given the necessary future changes in the Common Agricultural Policy;

- reducing acid deposition on soil and water by cutting sulphur dioxide emissions by 80% on 1980 levels by 2010;

- improving air quality by setting standards for the maximum level of each main pollutant (for example ozone) as set out in the national Air Quality Strategy;

- targets set out in the Biodiversity Action Plan, for example:

  - by 2010, restoring breeding otters to all river catchments and coastal areas where they have been recorded since 1960;

  - to identify and rehabilitate by the year 2000 the priority areas of existing reedbed (targeting those of 2 hectares or more) and maintain this thereafter by active management.

An important preliminary step to the development of targets can be the use of indicators which measure progress towards achieving policy objectives. In March 1996 we published a preliminary set of *Indicators of Sustainable Development*[3] to help interpret the large quantity of environmental information that is already available. Many of these indicators relate to processes of change and to environmental pressures in the countryside. Groups of indicators cover themes such as: Land Cover and Landscape, which includes indicators on pesticide usage and environmentally managed land; and Wildlife and Habitats, which includes indicators on native species at risk and lakes and ponds. The indicators can inform our policy response as well as helping householders, businesses, local planners, farmers and others to understand the impact which their own activities have on the environment. **We are committed to consulting widely on this preliminary set of indicators with a view to refining and consolidating a core set of indicators for publication in 1998.**

Chapter Four describes work which MAFF is undertaking to identify indicators which will monitor the environmental impact of certain agricultural practices.

Indicators of Sustainable Development for the United Kingdom

Indicator s1
Rural land cover

Arable and improved grassland cover predominate in lowland landscapes while heath/moorland and other semi-natural cover predominate in the uplands. Between 1984 and 1990, there were small net reductions in the area of arable land, improved grassland and heath/moorland cover in lowland landscapes partly because of increased urbanisation and afforestation. There was relatively little net change in upland landscapes; some improved grassland was converted to arable and there was a net loss of other semi-natural cover types, such as bracken.

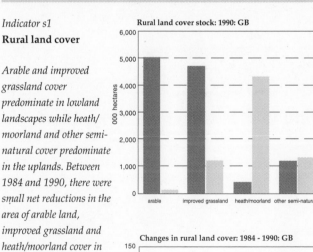

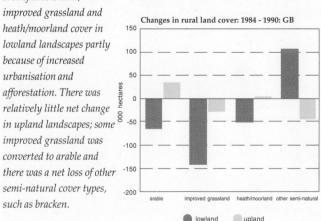

[3]*Indicators of Sustainable Development for the United Kingdom, HMSO*

Information

Rural England commits us to basing our policies on sound information. We consider that there is a particular need to improve our understanding of economic and social trends in the countryside. **The Rural Development Commission will therefore develop its research programme** with the aim of:

- improving data and indicators relating to rural deprivation;

- increasing understanding of the processes which cause people to fall into deprivation and to escape from it;

- repeating its national Survey of Rural Services in 1997, in cooperation with rural community councils and parish councils.

In addition, MAFF has initiated a programme of research which will focus on the relationship between agriculture and other rural economic activity. **Initial results will be available in 1997.**

We will examine how research and data can be used to provide more rural information as an aid to setting quantifiable and reasonable targets. We will consider whether information presently available can be made more accessible.

The Joseph Rowntree Foundation

The Joseph Rowntree Foundation is an independent non-political body which funds programmes of research and innovative development in the fields of housing, social care and social policy. While the Foundation has carried out a number of individual rural research projects, it has not until now dedicated an entire programme to rural concerns.

In the spring of 1996, the Foundation held a seminar on deprivation in rural areas to examine where it could contribute fresh thinking. The seminar recognised that the standard of living in rural areas has improved in many respects. However, for people on low incomes, or without access to transport, social exclusion can be felt more acutely than in urban areas. The elderly, young single people and single parents, for example, may be isolated from companionship and support. In addition, research funded by the Foundation in Scotland has found that the self reliance which characterises many long standing rural residents lowers their demands for support.

In June, the Foundation endorsed a new programme of research which will endeavour to pin down measurable facts about rural deprivation. Issues likely to be examined include:

- the cost of living in rural areas - for example how shop prices compare with those in urban areas, and whether there are additional essential expenses such as the need to maintain a car;

- income levels in the countryside, in order to compare rates of pay with urban employment; and

- the cost of delivering certain kinds of services, such as community care.

The first outputs from this programme are expected by late 1997.

LOCAL INITIATIVE AND VOLUNTARY ACTION

Local decision making is likely to be more responsive to local circumstances than uniform plans. We therefore aim to be sensitive to local concerns and to work in partnership with local people rather than impose top-down solutions.

Local Agenda 21

Many local authorities are working with businesses, voluntary organisations and community groups to identify what sustainable development means at the local level by preparing a Local Agenda 21. The Local Agenda 21 initiative arose from the Rio Earth Summit in 1992. At its heart is the principle that local action can not only improve the place in which we live but contribute globally to the achievement of sustainable development objectives.

In April 1996 the Countryside Commission, English Heritage and English Nature combined to publish *Ideas into Action for Local Agenda 21*, a source of information and ideas for community groups. It aims to encourage individuals and communities to develop a fuller understanding of their local environment, to influence decision making and to help shape the future of where they live and work.

Environment Agency

In order to help local authorities to develop their Local Agenda 21 activities, the Government Office for the South West sponsored a regional conference in November 1995. Participants emphasised the importance of improving access to information and sharing good practice, and concluded that a directory should be prepared to provide information about successful Local Agenda 21 initiatives in the region and sources of expertise. Plymouth City Council, sponsored by the Government Office, took the lead in preparing the directory, which was published in April 1996. *Keeping in Touch* covers all the local authorities in the South West. **The directory will be updated and expanded by the end of 1996. The conference will reconvene annually.**

An Environment Agency conservation officer in Kent participating in a local education initiative to make school children more aware of their environment.

Mendip Youth Initiatives

Mendip District Council in Somerset is actively involved in a series of Local Agenda 21 initiatives with a strong emphasis on young people. These will inform Mendip's Local Agenda 21 Strategy.

A Youth Summit held in autumn 1995 identified issues of concern to young people such as education, health, work and crime, and led to the development of several initiatives. One of these was the Postcard Project, which involved the distribution of a postcard sized questionnaire about young people's attitudes to the problems raised at the Summit. 2,500 responses were received, and were then discussed at the Mendip Summit in June 1996 which involved 120 people from all walks of life. The Postcard Project has now expanded and forged links with other schools in Britain and in Portugal and Belarus, allowing young people to compare their local environments and experiences.

Rural Action

Rural Action stimulates local initiative by rural communities to improve their quality of life. The Countryside Commission, English Nature and the Rural Development Commission together provide over £1 million annually to fund small projects and to support the work of volunteers. The scheme was introduced initially for three years in October 1992. Since then it has funded more than 2,300 community led projects in England and encouraged more than 50,000 days of volunteer labour. **We have agreed with the countryside agencies to continue funding up to 1998/99.**

Crediton Furniture Project, Devon

In March 1996 the Crediton Furniture Project formed a limited company with charitable status and began refurbishing donated household furniture and making it available to low-income families, the re-housed homeless and individuals leaving institutions and care. The project will also help to reduce fly-tipping and demand for landfill sites by providing a new outlet for unwanted furniture and support recycling initiatives in the district.

The initiative came from a group of people working through the local Volunteer Centre. A small Rural Action project grant funded a feasibility study which enabled the group to make a successful case for initial funding to Mid-Devon District Council.

THE VOLUNTARY SECTOR

Voluntary organisations are a vital part of voluntary activity in the countryside. They work across a wide spectrum of issues and in many different ways. They can be particularly effective in ensuring that we do not overlook the needs of disadvantaged people, for example in identifying and challenging the racism which people from ethnic minorities can experience in the countryside and in developing new and flexible ways of tackling problems.

Rural voluntary organisations vary greatly in size but generally are smaller than their counterparts in towns and have less staff. They also tend to be less specialist. This and their rural location can make it more difficult for them to access money, training and other support services. Rural community councils, councils for voluntary service, and national organisations are important sources of help for local rural voluntary organisations.

Since the publication of *Rural England* the Rural Development Commission has agreed to support a three-year programme of work by the National Council for Voluntary Organisations (NCVO) to increase the rural capability of national voluntary organisations and the money available for rural voluntary activity. **In consultation with NCVO we are considering how we might further encourage the rural voluntary sector.**

Make a Difference

The *Make a Difference* initiative has made a significant contribution to strengthening volunteering in rural areas as envisaged in *Rural England*. Of the 38 grants made since October 1995 to establish local volunteer development agencies, 18 were in rural or mainly rural district council areas. The 53 Volunteering Challenge grants awarded in October 1995 included four projects in rural areas and 19 projects covering both urban and rural areas. The Volunteering Partnership is taking account of the needs of rural areas in its work on its priority themes of carers and youth volunteering.

COMMUNITY INSTITUTIONS

Village and community halls play an important role in rural communities by providing a location for activities such as village meetings, child care, playgroups, over 60s and youth clubs and entertainment. Some are also used by doctors' surgeries, clinics, community shops, libraries and telecottages.

Many of England's 8,500 village halls are over 50 years old and are therefore not designed or equipped to conform to modern standards of hygiene, health and safety. Two new initiatives will help to enhance the capacity of village halls to meet the changing needs of rural communities:

- the Rural Development Commission has increased its support for improvements to village halls and community centres in 1996/97 from £850,000 to £1.2 million;

- in April 1996 Action with Communities in Rural England, with the support of the Rural Development Commission, won an award of £10 million from the Millennium Commission. The award, which will be matched by funding from local authorities and other bodies, will help to renovate approximately 180 village halls and to construct new flagship halls which will set 21st century standards of design, energy efficiency and access for people with disabilities.

The Churches

David Dixon

The Churches are a central focus of spiritual and community life in many rural communities. As a first step in identifying how the Government and others could work more closely with the Churches, the Rural Development Commission held a seminar in December 1995 with church representatives to discuss *Rural England* and its implications. **We will follow this with further discussions in autumn 1996.**

Parish Councils

Stockland Church in the Blackdown Hills

In *Rural England* we recognised the potential of parish councils to respond to the needs and priorities of local people and to represent their views, and we proposed to help parish councils develop their role in a number of ways. We have received nearly 600 responses to the proposals, over 90% from local councils, the large majority of which have been supportive. **We will therefore put forward proposals for legislation at the earliest opportunity, taking account of the results of the consultation.**

We proposed in *Rural England* to:

- Introduce legislation to establish a formal consultative framework between principal authorities and parish and town councils which will strengthen the consultative and representational role of local councils. Over 99% of the responses to this proposal gave it unqualified support. We have therefore consulted representative bodies on proposals for legislation and **will consult shortly on related guidance.**

▷
- Enable those parish councils which wish to do so to take on new responsibilities in community transport and crime prevention. These powers would not require parish councils to undertake new responsibilities but would provide new opportunities for those which wished to raise funds through the parish council precept to respond directly to local priorities. The overwhelming majority of respondents supported these proposals, although a small number objected to having to finance them from the parish precept. We are therefore preparing detailed proposals for legislation, which are described in Chapter Three.

▷
- Abolish the requirement for annual audit, subject to safeguards on accountability, for the smallest parish councils, for whom audit fees can represent an excessive burden. This proposal was supported by a narrow majority, but many councils feared a loss of accountability if the requirement for annual audit was removed. After more detailed consultation with the National Association of Local Councils, we have decided not to proceed with this proposal.

▷
- Encourage parish councils to play a more active role in the management of public access in their locality. 71% of respondents gave this proposal unconditional support, with a further 10% linking their support to the availability of additional funding. In July 1996 we therefore announced a new pilot project which will test ways of improving the management of footpaths, in particular by maximising the involvement of local people. This is described in more detail in Chapter Four.

▷
- Review current policy on setting up new parishes and, in particular, the criteria in DOE Circular 121/77[4]. We accept that the current system for changing parish arrangements has not worked well and that the opportunities for parish reviews have been curtailed. **We are therefore considering improvements to the system including changes to the guidance and will seek an early opportunity to legislate.**

▷ *Rural England* made clear our commitment that county and district authorities should honour their undertaking to improving consultation and devolving powers to parish councils. In August 1996, the Audit Commission published *Working Between the Tiers: Addressing The Issues*, which provides a checklist for action to improve working between different levels of local government. **We have asked the Audit Commission to review how the arrangements are working and to consider whether a guide to best practice might be appropriate.**

In addition we have given parish councils a new role in the management of National Parks in order to ensure representation of local concerns. **The Environment Act 1995 established new autonomous National Park Authorities, to include parish council representatives, which will take up their full range of powers on 1 April 1997.** The Act also gives the Authorities the new duty of seeking to foster the economic and social well-being of their local communities and aims to reduce conflicts between the Parks' purpose of conservation and recreation and the legitimate interest of those who live and work in the Parks.

▷ The Rural Development Commission and Cheltenham & Gloucester College of Higher Education have commissioned a study of parish council training needs and provision and **will discuss its conclusions with key organisations to identify priorities for further action.**

---

[4]*Circular 121/77 - 'Local Government Act 1972 Parish reviews' (12 December 1977)*

In March 1996, Hampshire Association of Parish and Town Councils organised the first National Youth Councils Conference in partnership with Hampshire County Council Youth Service. The two day residential conference attracted 160 delegates from all over England.

LOCAL AND NATIONAL GOVERNMENT

Local and national Government have a responsibility to be sensitive to the needs of rural communities. Rural strategies provide one useful mechanism for local authorities for identifying rural needs and responding to them with targeted policies. The Countryside Commission, English Nature and the Rural Development Commission, which jointly developed and promoted the approach in 1992, have undertaken a review of progress so far. A short study was used to inform a seminar for practitioners of rural strategies in April 1996. The study and seminar did not point to a need for further formal guidance to supplement that published jointly by the three agencies in 1992 but revealed:

● strong support for rural strategies to encourage an integrated approach to policies affecting the countryside;

● concerns about the quality of data available to underpin strategies, particularly on local economic performance;

● significant interest in the development of case study material to exemplify good practice and of a network to help practitioners share information.

In response, the three agencies are establishing a working group of practitioners to respond to the concerns raised at the seminar. It is important for strategies to be a living process in which a wide range of interest groups have a sense of ownership, for example by building on village appraisals. The group will therefore identify models for consulting local people and getting them actively involved in drawing up a strategy. The group will also seek to identify ways of broadening strategy development to embrace areas such as education, health and social services. **The group will aim to complete relevant case study material and other information during 1997.**

Cherwell Rural Strategy

Most rural strategies have been prepared at county level, but Cherwell in Oxfordshire is one of a small number of district councils to have taken the initiative. Publication of the strategy in November 1995 was the culmination of an extensive round of consultation, surveys and data collection. Parish councils were invited to participate through a comprehensive questionnaire and four workshop meetings, while Oxfordshire County Council and Oxfordshire Health were also closely involved.

Parish councils identified the following as significant problems facing their parishes:

- Safety and the impact of traffic   34%

- Retaining rural services   28%

- Low cost housing   26%

- Development pressures   26%

- Maintaining community spirit   26%

- Environmental problems   23%

- Adequacy of public transport   17%

The strategy contains an action programme to address these priorities, which draws on best practice from elsewhere in the country. Many actions are organisational rather than financial and relate to planning, social and health care, housing, leisure and economic development and to voluntary groups and the operation of parish councils. A rural development officer has been appointed to provide the focus for implementation of the action plan.

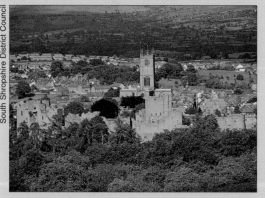

South Shropshire District Council

The inaugural meeting of the Ludlow Area Community Forum was on 23 October 1995 in the Assembly Rooms, Mill Street, Ludlow

South Shropshire Community Forums

South Shropshire District Council and Shropshire County Council have set up Community Forums based on the six market towns in South Shropshire. They held their first meetings during October and November 1995.

Each town provides a range of services to the surrounding rural areas. The Forums will enable views to be expressed by residents of the towns and the surrounding areas who use the towns. They give local people a new opportunity to influence the quality, quantity and priority of local services delivered by the local authorities and will enable the various tiers of local government and other agencies and interests to work together.

So far the Forums are starting to influence or react to:

- the Integrated Strategies for each of the six market towns;

- Local Service Plans;

- young people in rural areas;

- road maintenance and road repairs;

- traffic management issues;

- public rights of way and tourism issues.

Resources

It can be more expensive to deliver some services in sparsely populated parts of the country than in other areas, and the local government finance system is designed to make allowance for these additional costs.

Since publication of *Rural England* the Department of the Environment has commissioned research to examine how both sparsity and density of population affect the costs of providing local authority services. The projects were specified in close collaboration with the local authority associations. Final reports from the research were delivered in July 1996. **The research findings and the views of the local authority associations will inform our decisions on Standard Spending Assessments for 1997/98, which are used to calculate Revenue Support Grant for local authorities.**

The Department of Health is also researching the costs for health authorities of delivering certain health services in sparsely populated areas. This work is described in Chapter Three.

Local authorities themselves can generate additional spending resources by making the best use of their assets. In order to encourage all local authorities to develop coherent strategies for the future of county farms, *Rural England* announced the introduction of a two year scheme under the Private Finance Initiative, requiring only 10% of receipts from the sale of county farms to be used to redeem debt, thus giving increased spending power to those local authorities making disposals. We laid regulations in March 1996 enabling this scheme to come into effect on 1 April as planned, and making clear that the decision to retain or sell any farm is entirely at the discretion of the relevant local authority. We also issued guidance to local authorities in March 1996. This advised that the additional spending power made available to councils should be targeted on initiatives to improve the quality of life in rural areas. It emphasised the importance of responding to the identified needs and priorities of the area as a whole, consulting local interests as far as possible, and of supporting partnership arrangements involving the public, private and voluntary sectors.

Countryside Agencies

Our statutory countryside agencies, the Countryside Commission, English Nature and the Rural Development Commission, help to safeguard the economic, social and environmental interests of rural areas. Consistent with *Rural England*'s emphasis on dialogue and the reconciliation of competing priorities, the three agencies are committed to working more closely together so that they can better understand each others' perspectives and join forces where this will strengthen their impact.

The Chairmen of the three agencies meet regularly to ensure coordination of their work. English Nature and the Countryside Commission have agreed on a joint action plan for 1996/97 which provides for collaborative working on several projects, including the joint Character Map described in Chapter Four. The Rural Development Commission and the Countryside Commission are discussing areas for cooperative working, including planning, rural strategies, rural tourism and a variety of initiatives at local level. In conjunction with the Sports Council and the Environment Agency, the Countryside Commission is also formulating proposals for coordinating their work on countryside sport and recreation.

David Dixon

Hemyock Village

The Blackdown Hills: Devon and Somerset

The Blackdown Hills are characterised by a working landscape with distinctive geology, buildings and wildlife. Designated both as an Area of Outstanding Natural Beauty (AONB) and as a Rural Development Area, this is clearly a place where the Countryside Commission and the Rural Development Commission should work closely together to help enhance the landscape and economy of the area in ways which are mutually compatible.

The AONB designation in 1992 gave rise to local concern that the economic vitality of the area should not be compromised by the new emphasis on its landscape beauty. Through a newly appointed AONB officer and together with the local authorities, the two agencies initiated a community consultation which invited the people of the Blackdown Hills to develop their own management strategy for the area. They also helped to establish a Joint Advisory Committee, involving 21 members from local authorities, parish council associations, and bodies such as English Heritage, the National Farmers' Union and Devon and Somerset Wildlife Trusts. This and associated consultation led to a draft management strategy which was published for consultation in June 1996 and distributed widely - including to parish councils, libraries (including mobile libraries), tourist information points, village information points and post offices.

Following the closure of the consultation period at the end of September, the committee will present a revised strategy for adoption by the end of 1996. An annual action programme and conference will review achievement and monitor progress as well as providing an opportunity to raise new concerns.

The process pioneered in the Blackdown Hills is now being adopted in the nearby Mendip Hills and Quantock Hills AONBs.

Since publication of *Rural England* the countryside agencies have taken steps to strengthen their working relations with the Government Offices for the Regions in a number of ways to ensure that our regional programmes properly reflect rural concerns. The Rural Development Commission is reviewing its regional structure and is examining how it can best match the boundaries of other organisations including Government Offices. The Commission is also working more closely with the Business Link network, whose contracts are managed by Government Offices, in order to help sharpen the network's rural focus. These steps are described in Chapter Two.

Objective 5b Environmental Checklist

Rural England commits us to the principle that economic development in the countryside should take place in ways which protect and enhance the environment. In order to encourage this, the Countryside Commission and English Nature have begun to work with the Government Offices in certain regions to develop a strategic environmental dimension for their regional programmes.

In November 1995 the Countryside Commission put forward proposals to the Government Office for the North East for an environmental checklist which could be applied to bids for funding under the Northern Uplands Objective 5b programme. The final version of the checklist was approved in April 1996 and is now used to assess bids for European funding. The checklist evaluates whether projects have a positive, neutral or detrimental effect on the environment by reference to wildlife habitats, pollution, energy consumption, recycling and other criteria. Projects which demonstrate a positive impact are awarded extra points, which may help them to win funding in what is a competitive programme. In this way the checklist encourages project sponsors to develop an understanding of the needs of the environment at the start of the project development process, to examine ways of minimising any harmful environmental impact and to look for ways of providing positive environmental benefits.

Building on this approach, a Countryside Commission officer took up a placement with the Government Office European Team in August 1996.

Government Offices for the Regions

We are committed to integrating rural concerns properly into our national and regional policies. *Rural England* therefore charges the Government Offices for the Regions with meeting representatives of rural communities regularly and working more closely with the countryside agencies, the Forestry Commission and the regional organisation of MAFF. In its report of April 1996 the Environment Select Committee welcomed this commitment. The Government Offices have responded actively.

The Government Office for Eastern Region, for example, in partnership with the MAFF Regional Service Centre in Cambridge has established an Eastern Regional Board comprising countryside and other Government agencies. One of the Board's principal aims is to develop closer links with other bodies who operate in or serve rural communities. An early task for the Board was to organise a conference in June 1996 to debate and raise awareness of *Rural England* and to determine priorities for action within the Region. The conference was attended by over 100 people. The Government Office has also supported a number of other major regional conferences including one organised by Cambridgeshire County Council in Ely in February 1996, which gave the Council the remit of developing a rural strategy for the County.

Following publication of *Rural England* the Government Office for Yorkshire and Humberside formed a liaison group to identify work needed to implement the White Paper in the region and to ensure regular and effective coordination. The group, which includes representatives from MAFF, the Countryside Commission, English Nature, the Rural Development Commission and the Forestry Authority, played an important part in planning a conference in July 1996 to discuss factors affecting the quality of life in rural areas and shared priorities for the region.

The Government Office also commissioned research to identify key rural issues in the Yorkshire and Humberside region. The report analyses demographic and economic trends in the region's rural areas, evidence of rural deprivation, and a range of other issues such as housing, education and training, access to services and communications. It concludes by identifying priorities for rural development in the region including the key priority of ensuring that economic developments are sustainable so that the region's rural areas are both active and attractive. The Government Office published the report in June 1996 and presented it for discussion at the regional conference in July. The report's findings and the conclusions of the conference will help to guide the Government Office's strategic approach in the region.

In December 1995 the Government Office for the South West arranged a seminar to help develop a rural action programme for the region. Held in a village hall in Somerset, the seminar involved representatives from central and local government, education, industry, the police and conservation and community groups. Priorities identified for action by Government agencies in the South West include:

● action to promote best practice in market town regeneration in the South West;

● regional debates on the implications for the South West of the latest housing projections;

● regular meetings between the Government Office and rural agencies to discuss progress in implementing the principles and objectives set by *Rural England*;

● continuing involvement of the seminar members as a rural sounding group, and regular meetings of the group to discuss issues relevant to the rural South West.

While MAFF Regional Service Centres have a different and less strategic role from that of the Government Offices there are nevertheless many issues on which they need to co-ordinate their activities. In our response to the Environment Select Committee **we confirmed that we will ensure that the links between MAFF and the Government Offices continue to be strengthened and that the concerns of rural areas are given due weight in the development of policies for the regions.**

Government Offices and MAFF Regional Service Centres have therefore continued to develop those arrangements where liaison is crucial, such as Objective 5b programmes and the regional targeting of environmental land management programmes. Since the publication of *Rural England* arrangements to ensure that common interests and expertise are shared effectively have been further developed and enhanced. While the details vary from region to region, these commonly include MAFF participation in Government Office Regional Liaison Groups and Senior Management Team Meetings as well as Government Office participation in MAFF Regional Agri-Environmental Groups.

National Government

The process initiated by *Rural England* requires Government to give proper weight and consideration to rural concerns. This progress report, like *Rural England* last year, has been prepared by a joint team from DOE and MAFF. All Departments have monitored implementation of their commitments and considered what further measures may be justified. The Economic, Domestic and Environment Cabinet Committee, which was charged in *Rural England* with ensuring speedy progress in implementing commitments and with considering the rural dimension of policies across Government, has overseen the report's preparation. **We shall continue to ensure that national Government remains constantly alert to the rural dimension of all areas of policy.**

Hense Moor, Blackdown Hills

Listawood, Norfolk

North York Moors National Park

2. WORKING IN THE COUNTRYSIDE

Rural England made clear that the countryside has always been a place of work. It is our firm intention that it should remain so.

Our economic objectives for the countryside are to:

● maximise the competitiveness of rural businesses by creating the conditions for them to build on economic success and by helping to stimulate new and varied forms of wealth creation;

● encourage further diversification of rural enterprise so that local economies are less vulnerable to changes affecting any one particular sector; and

● do this in ways which respect, and where possible enhance, the environment.

Rural England recognised that rural enterprise had generally out-performed its urban equivalent and that the countryside had enjoyed higher growth in small firm formation and self employment, as well as lower levels of unemployment on average than urban areas. This remains the case. Between the winter of 1992/93 and that of 1995/96 employment grew by 3.6% in English rural local authority districts, compared with 3% in the country as a whole. In 1995, 4.5% of people of working age in rural areas were unemployed, compared with 6.3% in England as a whole [5]

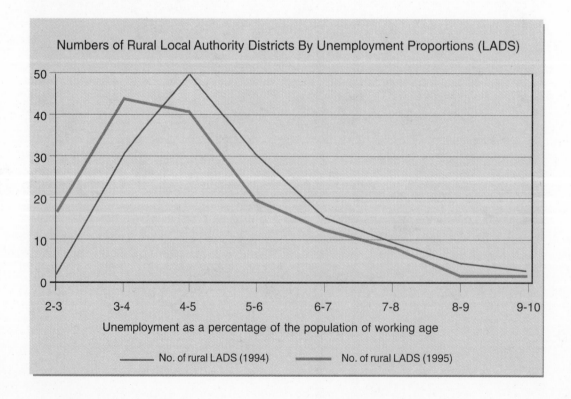

[5]*Figures are based on the claimant count*

Further improving the competitiveness of rural enterprise is primarily a matter for business itself. However, Government can also play a role by:

- creating the framework in which companies can prosper - for example maintaining low inflation, removing unnecessary regulatory burdens, and ensuring efficient communication and transport infrastructure;

- helping markets work better by providing direct assistance to enterprise in those rural areas which suffer from a concentration of economic and social problems.

The countryside's economic success is not uniform. Small firms in remoter and more inaccessible parts of the countryside tend to experience more constraints on business development and efficiency than those close to urban centres, and some areas are experiencing fundamental change in an economic sector on which they have relied heavily. In addition, published unemployment figures can mask local pockets of high unemployment as well as problems of under-employment, low rates of pay, seasonal work and the high cost of essential services such as transport. We therefore use targeted regeneration programmes to help areas with particular needs, and work with local partners to ensure that our programmes are tailored to meet locally defined priorities.

FRAMEWORK FOR ENTERPRISE

Planning

The planning system guides the development and use of land in the public interest and seeks to reconcile the twin objectives of development and environmental protection. During the year, we have continued to work to ensure that rural areas accommodate change and economic diversification, while continuing to protect the character of the countryside.

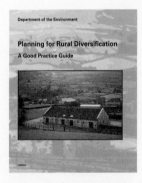

 In December 1995 we published *Planning for Rural Diversification: A Good Practice Guide*. This offers practical advice to local authorities on how to plan for development which both meets the economic and social needs of people in rural areas and respects the rural setting. It explains how they can more fully implement guidance in Planning Policy Guidance note 7 (PPG7) and provides examples of good practice.

Rural Business Use Class

 One way of overcoming concerns that, once granted planning permission, rural businesses might intensify beyond an acceptable level would be to introduce a new rural business class. In July 1996 we published a consultation paper[6] seeking views on this proposal. The proposal would not introduce new controls on existing rural businesses; but it would limit the intensity of traffic generated by proposed new rural businesses, so that, where desirable, a planning authority could grant planning permission with more confidence that subsequent intensification could be controlled. The consultation period has now ended and **we are considering what further action is appropriate in the light of responses received. We aim to announce our conclusion before the end of 1996.**

---

[6] *Consultation paper on the introduction of a new Rural Business Use Class into the Use Classes Order, DOE*

Planning Policy Guidance note (PPG) 7

In July 1996 we published a draft revision of PPG7, entitled *The Countryside - Environmental Quality and Economic Development*, for public consultation. Our proposals reflect the priorities established in *Rural England*, and the results of a recent research project[7]. Compared with existing guidance, the main changes proposed are:

- new advice on achieving good quality development and respecting the character of the countryside;

- clarification of the agricultural importance of grade 3a land within the policy of protecting the best and most versatile land;

- greater discrimination in favour of business rather than residential use on the re-use of rural buildings;

- new emphasis on the importance of thoroughly checking the lawfulness of developments under agricultural permitted development rights, and proposing to amend the Town and Country Planning (General Permitted Development) Order 1995 to make it possible in certain circumstances to require the removal of new buildings erected under these rights but no longer used for agriculture;

- new measures to counter abuse of the concession which allows houses for farm workers to be built in the open countryside so that new permanent farm dwellings should be allowed only if the agricultural unit has been established for at least five years, has been profitable for at least three of them, is currently financially sound, and has a clear prospect of remaining so; and

- advice on local countryside designations and on the planning implications of Rural Development Areas and Objective 5b areas.

We intend to publish an updated version of PPG7 in early 1997.

Sport and Leisure

Recognising the increasingly diverse demands for rural leisure activities, we have commissioned research into the effectiveness of PPG17, which provides advice on meeting the sport and recreation needs of both residents and visitors. The project will include a study of leisure activities which can be noisy and obtrusive. We expect to publish the research results in 1997.

Cricket at Thornton Hough, Cheshire

Guidance on Out-of-Town Shopping

In June 1996, to emphasise the importance of enhancing the viability and vitality of town centres, we issued revised planning policy guidance on retail developments (PPG6). The guidance recognises the potential vulnerability of market towns to out-of-town superstores and stresses that such developments should be of an appropriate scale, and preferably located in, or at the edge of, the town centre. In order to protect important rural services, proposals for farm shops and shops in rural petrol stations should take account of the likely impact on nearby village shops, and the inclusion of pharmacies and post offices in out-of-centre developments will be discouraged.

[7] *Planning Controls over Agricultural and Forestry Development and Rural Building Conversions, DOE, December 1995*

User Friendly Appeals System

It is important that the planning system is accessible and that applications and appeals are settled with the minimum delay. In September 1996, following consultation, we published a new circular on procedures[8]. This emphasised the advantages of using informal hearings rather than inquiries to deal with appeals, the value of pre-inquiry meetings, and our wish to see tighter control over cross-examination at inquiries.

Design

Where development is unavoidable, sensitive design and high quality building can help to minimise the impact of new buildings. This is discussed further in Chapter Four. The principles of good design were endorsed in a new draft of PPG1 *General Policy and Principles*, issued in August 1996. **We intend to publish a revised version of PPG1 early in 1997.**

DEREGULATION

Regulations are necessary to protect the public and the environment by establishing minimum standards. However, small firms, which predominate in the countryside, can suffer disproportionately from unnecessary red tape. Our Deregulation Initiative aims to ensure that legislation is limited to what is really necessary to protect the public and the environment.

In March 1996, in response to concerns raised by small businesses, we announced a new computer system to provide information on forms and regulations. A prototype system has been developed, and following trials, discussions on future work (including financing arrangements) are taking place with the private sector. **We aim to announce further action in 1997.** In spring 1996, we also introduced new requirements for all legislative proposals affecting businesses to be accompanied by Regulatory Appraisals, including Risk Assessments and Compliance Cost Assessments (CCAs).

In January 1996, we relaxed restrictions on signposting so that direction signs may now be used for many more types of rural businesses, such as hotels, pubs and restaurants. The Department of Transport is also reviewing the current arrangements for naming other commercial premises, such as shops and superstores, on traffic signs and published a consultation paper[9] in June 1996. **We aim to bring forward legislative amendments in the first half of 1997.**

Rural pubs make a valuable contribution to village social life and are an important part of rural tourism. However, in some areas they are under increasing threat of closure. Under proposed new arrangements for discretionary rate relief (described in more detail in Chapter Three), local authorities will be able to reduce rates bills for rural shops and businesses, including pubs, which they consider to be of value to the community.

The Agricultural Tenancies Act 1995 encourages landowners to offer more land for rent by providing a simplified legal framework. Initial indications suggest that a significant number of new farm business tenancies have already been agreed under this deregulated approach. Landlords and tenants have been able to use this new freedom to negotiate agreements covering a variety of types of holding, a length of term which suits their particular needs, and a wider range of activities within a single tenancy than was possible previously. This will benefit both the agriculture industry and the wider rural economy. **We intend to announce the results of an initial evaluation of the effects of the Act in 1997.**

---

[8] *Planning Appeal Procedures, DOE*
[9] *Revision of the Traffic Signs Regulations and General Directions 1994, DOT*

Rural Business Unit

Rural England committed us to consider whether commercial activities associated with a rural estate should be assessed as a single trading unit for tax purposes. The case for the Rural Business Unit has been considered, however, any tax measure which treats the lettings activities of rural landlords differently from those of their urban counterparts could cause considerable difficulties. Equally, extending the Rural Business Unit concept to all landlords, which has also been considered, would be extremely costly in revenue terms. The Government does not therefore plan to take these proposals any further.

BUSINESS SUPPORT

Training and advice are important for the success of businesses wherever they are located. However, rural firms, because of their small size or because of their distance from major centres, can sometimes have difficulty in gaining access to these services.

Rural firms, no less than those in towns and cities, should have ready access to training and advice services. We are therefore taking further steps to ensure that Training and Enterprise Councils (TECs) and Business Links, which are the principal providers of these services to businesses throughout England, take full account of the needs of rural businesses when drawing up their programmes and that they respond flexibly to local, including rural, priorities.

Business Links

Business Links provide one-stop shops for businesses in need of training, advice and information. *Rural England* set us the target of establishing 200 Business Links in England by the end of 1995. By August 1996, 232 had opened. **We aim to complete national coverage by the end of 1996, although a "tail" of very small outlets and access points will continue to open into 1997.**

In June 1996 we published a consultation document on a new approach to Business Support[10]. This emphasises the importance of partnership in the design and delivery of business support and of tailoring this support to meet the needs of individual business customers. In order to provide rural firms with clear and well resourced assistance, Business Links are:

- increasingly focusing their services on the needs of rural companies; and

- working closely with the Rural Development Commission, which has already entered into joint working arrangements with 25 Business Links in Rural Development Areas.

We shall work with Business Link partners to ensure that such joint working arrangements, including joint branding of services, are extended to all Business Links in Rural Development Areas as early as possible in 1997.

In order to ensure that our business support resources achieve the maximum possible impact, we proposed to apply more widely the challenge funding approach already adopted in the Single Regeneration Budget (SRB) and Rural Challenge by bringing together support for small and medium sized businesses into a local competitiveness budget, worth around £200 million a year. Most of this budget would continue to be allocated through the Government Offices' contracts with TECs, to ensure a consistent level of business support across the country. However, up to 25% would be made available on a challenge basis to the most effective partnership bids.

---

[10] *Helping Businesses to Win: Consultation on a New Approach to Business Support, Cabinet Office*

The consultation document invited views from rural businesses on whether they would wish to see the challenge approach applied to the Rural Development Commission's business support services. Under this proposal the Commission would eventually contribute up to 25% of its business support expenditure (£3.8 million in 1996/97) to the challenge fund. The Commission's contribution would be reserved for the best bids from partnerships in Rural Development Areas. In addition, the Commission, in partnership with relevant Business Links, would have the opportunity to bid for resources in support of rural enterprise from this local challenge fund.

The consultation closed in September 1996. **We shall announce our conclusions in October.**

We are also seeking to foster good working relations between Business Links and MAFF. In order to provide Business Links and their customers with a wide range of information on MAFF's role in relation to farming and food businesses, **MAFF will issue an information pack to all Business Links in England before the end of 1996.**

Training and Enterprise Councils (TECs)

It is important that the Government funded programmes delivered by TECs are designed with the flexibility to be effective in a rural context.

In January 1996, in response to the publication of *Rural England*, the Consortium of Rural TECs (CORT) held a seminar for member TECs to consider ways in which they could influence the development of policies, both nationally and locally, in order to benefit rural areas. In addition to planning, support for small businesses, transport and service delivery, the seminar considered:

● the need for research to identify the costs of delivery of services in rural areas;

● ways to disseminate good practice;

● the possibility of developing credit unions among TECs;

● the scope for greater liaison with other agencies, such as the Rural Development Commission;

● the role of "Parish Ambassadors", as piloted by Cumbria TEC;

● developing a rural TEC checklist, based on the Rural Charter Checklist.

Rural Growth Fund: Finance for Small Businesses in Cornwall

Launched in March 1996, the Rural Growth Fund is financed by Lloyds Bank and the Rural Development Commission to provide loans for businesses in rural areas of Cornwall and the Isles of Scilly. The Fund responds to a common problem of small rural firms by offering help to those seeking to expand who have encountered difficulty in raising all the finance they need from traditional sources, such as banks, because of lack of security or limited track record. Whilst the objective of the Fund is to facilitate the expansion of smaller, established businesses, new ventures will also be considered if they will create jobs.

Loans have already provided investment in computer equipment, premises, additional staff, and, in one case a new vehicle for a company which provides specialised travel packages in Cornwall.

Self Employment in Rural Areas

In Rural Development Areas (RDAs), around 20% of the workforce is self employed, compared with 12% in England as a whole. In order to consider how best to give further encouragement to self employment and business start ups, we have carried out an evaluation to assess the experience of self employed people in rural areas. The evidence gathered, from the Rural Development Commission, academic researchers, and others, confirms that people starting in business in rural areas generally do not face greater obstacles than those elsewhere. However, in remoter rural areas people do seem to be at a relative disadvantage, particularly in their access to information, advice and guidance, compared with other parts of the country.

We have therefore invited CORT and the Commission to develop a number of initiatives which will enhance the potential for rural areas to generate and support self-employment. **In the autumn of 1996, they will arrange a conference for TECs and their partners to discuss effective strategies for promoting self employment in rural areas.** This will be followed by a series of demonstration projects to develop innovative local good practice and a guide outlining help available through TECs, further education colleges, Business Links and other agencies. To supplement this, in January 1997, the Department for Education and Employment will highlight the needs of the self employed, especially in RDAs, in guidance to Government Offices.

Rural Development Commission/Jon Stone

The Swanage Advice Shop for Young People opened in January 1996 in response to local concerns about the seasonal nature of employment, low pay, and poor transport links to training facilities and Jobcentres in Bournemouth and Poole. It brings together services from many partners, including careers advice, health services, Citizens Advice Bureau, and a new Jobcentre

Overcoming Barriers to Job Interviews

The Employment Service continues to explore new ways of helping people in rural areas to find jobs. Since September 1996 South Norfolk and Waveney district, along with others, has been involved in further developing the Jobseekers Grant. This is designed to help long term unemployed people to overcome barriers to getting job interviews, and aims to provide practical assistance, such as suitable interview clothing, relevant certification (for example, to comply with food hygiene requirements) and registration with professional bodies, and help with travel costs for interviews. A project along similar lines will start in Devon in October 1996.

Rural Development Commission/Rob Cousins

Childcare

In 1993, in recognition of the importance of childcare for parents wishing to return to work, we set the target of creating an additional 42,000 after-school and holiday childcare places for school age children in England by the end of March 1996. TECs exceeded this target by 46%, creating some 61,000 places in England including rural areas.

In November 1995 we committed a further £12.5 million for investment in out-of-school childcare for three years from April 1996. This brings the total invested in out-of-school childcare close to £60 million since 1993. We expect TECs to have created more than 80,000 childcare places in England by 1999.

Wickwar, Gloucestershire

In July 1996, the Rural Development Commission published a practical guide to *Developing Rural Childcare*. The Commission will also support a new rural project run by the National Council for Voluntary Childcare Organisations and Action with Communities in Rural England. Launched in February 1996, the initiative will promote a more strategic approach to childcare provision at a local level and develop new partnerships between the statutory and voluntary sectors.

Telecommunications and Information Technology

Telecommunications and information technology offer new opportunities for rural enterprise, but will only be fully exploited if high quality services and training are available.

▷ The Rural Development Commission's study into telecommunications infrastructure[11] found no evidence that rural areas are disadvantaged in accessing basic telephone services. However, they are less well served by Integrated Services Digital Network (ISDN), which provides higher capacity and faster data transmission. The study confirmed the importance of remoter rural areas continuing to have access to the basic telephone service on the same charges basis as the rest of the country despite differences in the cost of providing the service.

▷ Developments in wireless technology have the potential to increase high quality connections in remote rural areas, as an alternative to expensive land-line improvements, and in February 1996 the Department of Trade and Industry awarded two licences to provide fixed wireless (or radio fixed access) services at 2GHz in defined remote rural areas. In England these cover upland parts of the north, the Welsh Borders and parts of the south west. Services are expected to begin in late 1997.

▷ A further Commission study[12] reviewed the likely impact of teleworking on rural areas. It identified opportunities for the development of new telemediated services, such as shopping, banking and entertainment, and a greater expansion of freelance work in areas where ISDN is available. The study highlighted a need for more information on the extent of different forms of teleworking and their multiplier effect on local economies. **The Commission will consider, with the Office for National Statistics, ways of improving the availability of information on rural teleworking.**

In autumn 1996 the Commission will publish a good practice guide on the establishment and management of rural telecottages.

Cumbria Credits - Adult Education and Training

This seven year scheme seeks to broaden the skills base, by using advanced information technology to combat the problems traditionally faced by those who live in remoter areas and who wish to train or expand their skills. In order to improve accessibility, especially amongst those without transport or who might be deterred by distant educational establishments, the project is centred in local primary schools and uses the latest in distance learning techniques.

Led by the local education authority, and involving, amongst others, the County Council, Cumbria TEC, local employers such as BT and Olivetti, and Voluntary Action Cumbria, the scheme will receive £8.5 million from the SRB Challenge Fund over seven years. This is expected to draw in over £11 million of other funding. The scheme will help 4,300 people to obtain qualifications, provide 1,800 childcare places, and create or safeguard over 800 jobs.

---

[11] *Developments in Telecommunications Infrastructure and the Potential Effects on Rural Areas, RDC, 1996*
[12] *Teleworking and Rural Development, RDC, 1996*

GOVERNMENT AND EUROPEAN PROGRAMMES

Government and European regeneration programmes provide direct assistance to encourage the development of new enterprises in run down areas. Some programmes operate nationwide while others are targeted on specific rural areas.

The Single Regeneration Budget (SRB) Challenge Fund is the Government's main instrument for encouraging local regeneration in England. In the first two bidding rounds, the Challenge Fund approved over 70 schemes which are directly targeted on rural areas. These will attract over £180 million in Challenge Fund support, with complementary private and other public investment. We are currently considering bids submitted for the third round; **we hope to announce winners by the end of 1996.**

Amble

In December 1995 the Amble Challenge won SRB funds of £345,000 to support the regeneration of this former coal exporting and fishing town on the Northumberland coast. The total cost of the scheme is £3.9 million.

The project is led by a partnership which includes the District and County Councils, Warkworth Harbour Commission, Amble Town Council, Amble Business Club, the Community Council of

Northumberland and the Multi Agency Crime Prevention Initiative. It combines measures to diversify the local economy with environmental and infrastructure improvements concentrating on the town centre and harbour area.

The derelict Fourways public house, built as a hotel in the 1850s when the coal export trade was expanding rapidly, will be converted into the headquarters for the Amble Development Trust Partnership. In the long term, the community is working to establish a Heritage and Craft Centre, a theatre, and a museum which will relate Amble's unique history of sea and coal.

Rural Challenge

The Rural Challenge competition continues to encourage innovative projects which will make a significant impact on economic and social problems in Rural Development Areas. When assessing bids, we give priority to those which demonstrate a high level of community involvement and which best respect or enhance the environment. In November 1995, the Rural Development Commission awarded a total of £6 million to the winners of the second round, which are expected to lever in nearly £20 million from other sources over the next three years. **We shall announce the results of the third round of the competition in November 1996.**

 We will review Rural Challenge in 1997/98, in order to evaluate its success and draw lessons for the future.

Eco-Tech Swaffham

In the second round of Rural Challenge proposals to help regenerate the small market town of Swaffham in Norfolk through the development of a new Eco-Tech Centre won £1 million. Over a three year period the project will:

- reclaim a derelict industrial site to create a business park for new and innovative firms related to the environment;

- attract visitors by demonstrating a range of environmentally-friendly technology;

- develop education and training programmes for the local community;

- create up to 47 new jobs and provide training for around 400 people.

Rural Challenge prize money has helped the partnership, which includes Breckland District Council, the local TEC, and three private sector firms, to attract around £7 million from European funding, the County Council and commercial sponsorship.

In its report on *Rural England* published in April this year, the House of Commons Environment Select Committee accepted that competitive funding was an effective way of allocating resources between competing priorities. We remain committed to challenge funding as a means of encouraging local people to devise solutions to local problems.

It is encouraging that many of the partnerships which have not been successful in competitive funding programmes have nevertheless been able to pursue elements of their schemes using funds from other sources.

Creswell, Derbyshire

Creswell is a community whose life was coal for three quarters of a century. The impact of colliery closures on the local economy was serious, and the miners' welfare building, which was severely damaged by fire in August 1994, is a symbol of the decline and decay which threatens the village. In 1995 a Rural Challenge bid proposed converting the building to provide office units, community and training facilities, changing rooms for nearby sports grounds, and a creche. Although the bid was not selected for a Rural Challenge prize, the Creswell Regeneration Trust has secured nearly £500,000 of private and public sector funding to develop the site, which will be an important practical step towards community regeneration.

The District of Bolsover

European Funding

European funding makes a major contribution towards rural regeneration, particularly since the review of eligible areas in 1993. This substantially increased the rural areas in England which could receive funding. Under the Objective 5b programme the European Union has allocated over £400 million to designated rural areas in England between 1994-99, to strengthen and diversify rural economic activity. Measures which have been supported under the current programmes include:

● development of new and existing businesses;

● provision of infrastructure;

● encouraging tourism through the promotion and development of new attractions, accommodation and improved access;

● training and capacity building for local people; and

● environmental enhancement and conservation.

The European Union's contribution will be more than doubled by matching funding from other sources, such as local and national Government, TECs and the voluntary and private sectors.

Vindolanda Open Air Museum, Northumberland

The Vindolanda Open Air Museum in Northumberland won a European Regional Development Fund (ERDF) grant of £126,000 under the Northern Uplands Objective 5b programme in order to improve the museum and increase visitor numbers. Total project costs were over £330,000.

This scheme, which was completed in March 1996, forms part of the management strategy for the World Heritage Site of Hadrian's Wall in Northumberland. It consists of a series of full-scale reproductions of Roman buildings and other structures on the site of the original Roman fort. The other contributors to the project are the Vindolanda Trust and the Museums and Galleries Commission.

As well as creating a stimulating tourist attraction and increasing visitors to the museum, the project has created 10 new jobs and safeguarded 13 more.

The LEADER II for England programme which was approved in summer 1995, will provide a further £21 million up to the end of 1999. It is targeted at specific communities within Objective 5b areas and will support small scale, innovative projects not normally assisted under Objective 5b.

The Challenge for Agriculture

Within the Objective 5b programme, Challenge for Agriculture provides targeted support for farming communities, helping to create and sustain employment in these areas. Since spring 1995 over 300 applications have been received, and of these nearly 90 have been approved to date. Total expenditure on projects funded is in the order of £30 million, of which nearly £8 million and £7 million have come from the European Union and MAFF respectively. Projects supported have covered a wide range of activities and include the provision of business support and consultancy services, food marketing initiatives, farm diversification, support for the development of alternative energy (biomass) crops, woodland, horticulture, farm tourism and the environment.

In order to assist applicants in developing project ideas, we have provided "facilitators" in each of the eligible areas. Facilitators will help to ensure that projects meet the regional strategic objectives, and, if necessary, will co-ordinate similar or complementary schemes into a single package. They will also provide guidance on preliminary studies and funding arrangements.

Regeneration of the North York Moors

MAFF and European Union funding are contributing over £1.5 million towards moorland regeneration in the North York Moors National Park. Approved in December 1995, this is the first collaborative attempt in the Moors to tackle the bracken and associated disease problems which affect both the sheep and grouse on which the local economy depends. These have resulted in a disastrously low level of productivity - for example, lamb rearing rates are only around two-thirds of what might be achieved if the chronic tick infestation could be eradicated.

North York Moors National Park

Egton Moor

A strong partnership of interests from the farming, landowning and conservation sectors has developed a concerted four year programme of improvements. A sheep health scheme has wide support; the bracken, which has progressively invaded the heather moorland, and acts as a reservoir for tick borne viruses, will be controlled; habitats for ground nesting birds will be re-created; and a marketing plan has been drawn up for the increased output of grouse and lambs. The project will strengthen the moorland economy - benefits will extend to other local businesses involved in agricultural services. 28 additional jobs will be created and over 155 jobs safeguarded by the project.

2. WORKING IN THE COUNTRYSIDE

SECTORAL INDUSTRIES

Agriculture

Excluding the crops we cannot grow here, our farmers and growers produce about three quarters of the food and animal feed consumed in the United Kingdom. In addition to providing direct employment for some 2% of the workforce, they contribute around 1.5% to GDP and form the basis for a dynamic food and drink sector which employs around 450,000 people.

Labour force on Agricultural Holdings in England ('000s)				
	1973	1994	1995	change 1973-1995
total labour force	n.a.	430.9	425.2	n.a.
total labour force, excluding spouses	517.5	381.7	378.8	-27%
full time farmers, partners, active directors	150.9	111.5	110.0	-27%
part time farmers, partners, active directors	41.1	72.2	73.0	+78%
salaried managers	5.3	6.9	6.7	+26%
total other workers	320.1	191.0	189.1	-41%

The number of agricultural holdings in England continues to fall - from 172,000 in 1976 to 146,000 in 1995 (a decrease of 4.5% from 1994). Only 86,000 are considered to be full time, and they account for 98% of agricultural output. The trend towards specialisation and away from mixed farming continues.

Reform of the Common Agricultural Policy, which will have both economic and environmental implications is covered in Chapter Four.

We recognise that BSE has had a major impact on the agricultural sector and the wider rural economy and that, for the foreseeable future, many of those working there will be affected by the impact of the disease and its associated control and eradication measures. This applies not only to beef and dairy farmers but equally to those employed in ancillary sectors, such as livestock markets, haulage, slaughtering and processing. The programmes introduced to underpin essential elements of the sector and the other support measures agreed within the European Union will go some way towards offsetting the economic losses suffered by individuals and businesses. The losses to the wider economy, arising principally from unmarketable beef and the costs of disposal, will though continue to be large. In addition to the economic effects, many of our rural landscapes and habitats depend on continued extensive grazing by cattle.

The stringent measures adopted to safeguard public and animal health and to restore consumer confidence, combined with the framework for ending the European Union export ban, should help to bring an increasing degree of normality to the market. They will contribute to restoring the prospects of those whose livelihoods depend on the beef sector and to preserving valuable landscapes and habitats.

Nevertheless, whatever support measures are in place, it is clear that radical adaptation and possibly contraction of the beef industry will inevitably result. **In consultation with the countryside agencies, we will monitor the effects on habitats which are dependent in some degree on grazing cattle.**

It appears that the number of job losses and redundancies are small in relation to the size of the job market as a whole. The increase in claims for unemployment and income support attributable to BSE was 5,542 in the period to the end of July 1996.

We have agreed a framework within which Government Offices, TECs and the Employment Service, who are responsible for quantifying the effects of BSE on local communities and responding to emerging needs, can work together to ensure that appropriate services are available to help individuals, businesses and communities. This may include measures to assist individuals who have lost their jobs, guidance for businesses which face different patterns of demand and, in some cases, innovative projects to regenerate local economies.

Rural Stress

We recognise with concern that farmers and agricultural workers are among the occupational groups with the highest rate for suicide. The Rural Stress Information Network, which includes representatives from the Churches, the National Farmers Union, the Royal Agricultural Society of England, and the Samaritans, disseminates information on the extent and effects of stress in rural communities and promotes and co-ordinates initiatives to alleviate rural stress. These initiatives include the establishment of voluntary rural stress helplines, which currently operate in thirty English counties. The helplines have been particularly effective in relation to concerns over BSE.

Agricultural Education and Training

Rural England emphasised the need for flexible and responsive education and training arrangements for new entrants to the agriculture and horticulture industries, for existing workers and for those moving to new areas of business. In spring 1996, following a review of the arrangements for providing Industry Training Organisation (ITO) and Lead Body services for the agricultural and commercial horticulture sectors, MAFF let a further contract, worth up to £1.9 million, for one year with ATB-Landbase. The contract includes measures to raise the profile of training by promoting the benefits which businesses can derive from it and for ensuring that the quality of instructors registered with ATB-Landbase is maintained and that their technical knowledge is kept up-to-date. **Following discussions with ATB-Landbase and other interested organisations, we are aiming to announce future support arrangements for training in the agriculture and horticulture industries in the autumn of 1996.**

In rural areas where remoteness can significantly affect training uptake it is important to ensure all training opportunities are fully explored. The agricultural colleges remain popular places to study, providing a diverse range of courses tailored to local needs, full-time and part-time, for students and adults alike. A consortium of 22 agricultural colleges have developed flexible learning methods which will especially benefit trainees in remoter areas who find it difficult to travel to a college. The colleges have jointly produced self-teach material, which has been available since April 1996. They hope to build on this initiative to develop "Distance Learning" material that will further assist people in rural areas to improve their skills through study.

Farm Tourism

Farmers are increasingly seeking to maximise the use of their buildings and other resources and looking beyond the production of food to alternative sources of income. Diversification can take many forms, from traditional bed and breakfast to film locations and offering a picturesque alternative to the registry office for civil marriage services. Farm tourism is an important part of the Challenge for Agriculture Objective 5b programme. In March 1996, in order to emphasise the importance of offering a recognised quality product, MAFF, the English Tourist Board and the Farm Holiday Bureau, launched a series of events designed to highlight the benefits of grading farm accommodation.

MAFF has also helped to set up Farm Attraction Groups to develop farms as tourist attractions. Since the publication of *Rural England*, Groups have been set up in Cambridgeshire, Hertfordshire and North London, County Durham, Sussex, the Marches area and the Wessex area. There are now 20 groups covering 22 counties in England.

Farm Holiday Bureau Hits the Net

To attract visitors from overseas, the Farm Holiday Bureau has developed an Internet Service. Potential visitors can browse through information displayed in map form, or search by using key words. Over 4,000 enquiries were received in the first three months since the launch in May 1996.

Tourism is covered in greater detail on pages 39 - 41.

Alternative Crops

Crops which provide raw materials for industry and energy can be an attractive alternative for farmers to conventional crops. They can also contribute to our wider sustainable development objectives and help increase local employment opportunities.

In March 1996 MAFF published the National Biomass Energy Strategy, which sets out our plans over the next five years for encouraging renewable energy production from crops such as short rotation coppice and by-products such as straw and chicken litter. The Strategy aims to help industry and Government work together to develop energy from biomass, and help meet our target of creating 1,500 megawatts of new electricity generating capacity from renewable resources by the year 2000.

MAFF has organised a variety of events designed to increase the use of crops for industrial and energy purposes. These include a national seminar in May 1996 to explore the possibilities for using vegetable oils as lubricants, and a workshop in Yorkshire in June for farmers interested in growing short rotation coppice for the power generation market. MAFF has also supported the construction of alternative crop projects for a variety of industrial purposes, including two processing plants producing flax fibre. One plant opened in Dorset in August 1996; the other, in Cornwall, will open in autumn 1996.

As part of our policy to promote collaborative research between industry and the research community, we announced a new LINK programme on renewable raw materials in June 1996. This five-year programme, funded jointly by industry and Government, will commission research to overcome the barriers to the uptake of alternative crop products by potential end-users in a wide variety of industrial sectors.

The Marches Dwarf Hop Company

Traditionally grown hops are in steady decline, and prices offered are often below the cost of production. Although demand for the high quality "aroma" hops remains steady, their production is threatened by an incurable soil disease. Dwarf hops, developed by the UK hop breeding programme, offer the potential to increase the supply of quality hops sought by the brewers.

The Marches Dwarf Hop Company is co-ordinating the efforts of a number of Herefordshire farmers to establish the world's first centre of excellence for dwarf hopgrowing. Farmers will be injecting £12 million into the local economy over the next ten years. The project plans to plant 250 hectares of dwarf hops by the year 2000, and will give growers full support through research, training and advice. It will also bolster the order books of over 30 small businesses. As dwarf hops grow to only half the height of traditional varieties, much of the investment required is for new machinery, to which Challenge for Agriculture Objective 5b has contributed £700,000.

Food

In 1995, the value of UK exports of food and drink increased to some £10 billion, an increase of £1 billion on the previous year. This represents 6% of the total value of our exports.

Supported jointly by the Agriculture Departments and the industry, Food From Britain (FFB) puts food producers in direct contact with foreign customers. In December 1995, FFB opened a new representative office in Denmark; it now supports nine overseas offices in Europe, North America and Japan. **FFB's corporate strategy for the next three years envisages expanding the coverage of its existing offices and extending their services into Eastern Europe as well as the Middle East.**

Regional speciality food and drink groups are a valuable marketing tool for assisting small, rurally based enterprises to promote their products, develop their businesses and create jobs in the countryside. In January 1996, two new groups were set up with the help of Government funding. *Middle England Fine Foods* and *Tastes of the South East* have joined three other regional and several more local groups.

Cornish King

The Cornish King logo, launched in June 1996, with assistance from Challenge for Agriculture Objective 5b funding, the Cornwall Tourist Board, and other local partners, will draw together Cornish fruit and vegetable producers and packers behind a quality trademark. Membership is open to all packhouses who can meet the quality standards. The horticulture industry in the Objective 5b area has a revenue of over £70 million, and employs at least 2,500 people. Co-operative marketing of a quality branded product, attractive to retailers, will increase returns and strengthen the wider economy.

Westbury Blake

The Stilton Cheesemakers Association identified the USA as a significant potential market, and in July 1996, the Association's accredited producers embarked on a new "exports to the USA" project with assistance from MAFF's Market Task Force.

In addition to wider Government policies to develop competitiveness, we aim to foster the efficiency of the food and drink industries by helping individual businesses, groups and trade bodies to improve their marketing performance, and by disseminating best practice through seminars and conferences. Help towards improved marketing and management is available under the Marketing Development Scheme. Since 1992, over £10 million worth of grants have been awarded to more than 200 companies and trade bodies, for feasibility studies, employment of professional marketing staff and access to training and expert advice.

The horticulture industry, which employs over 100,000 people in England, is an important source of employment in many rural areas. In order to provide growers with the information and support they need to develop exports, the horticulture industry has set up an export bureau. Established in partnership between Government and industry, the bureau opened for business in July 1996, and will focus initially on salad crops and field vegetables.

Forestry

Forestry contributes to enterprise, especially in remote rural areas, through timber production and through non-timber activities such as tourism. The Forestry Commission's survey of forestry employment in Great Britain in 1993/94 (published in December 1995) showed that over half of those employed in forestry (19,400 people) were in England. Various initiatives are underway to develop this small but important source of employment especially in remote rural areas.

The construction industry is a major user of timber. In February 1996, we published *Timber 2005* which set out a ten year research programme for the use of timber, based on consultation with the construction industry. This aims to increase the sustainable use of timber, and will help to create markets for domestic products.

Many of England's woodlands have been left unmanaged, and much of the timber they produce is of low quality. To help stimulate new uses for this timber, and thus increase its value, we funded research by the Parnham Trust and Bath University on the utilisation of low grade timber in buildings. The Parnham Trust has built a house to accommodate students at Hooke Park College in Dorset, using this research, which was completed in spring 1996; further buildings are planned.

The house for 8 students at Hooke Park built with low grade timber from the estate. The grass roof provides insulation.

One of the key features of effective woodland management is sound marketing of timber, but opportunities for marketing from smaller woodlands can prove elusive. *Woodlots*, a magazine launched in 1994 by the Forestry Authority and East Sussex County Council, allows growers to advertise in a format which can be widely circulated to buyers. Circulation has steadily increased, and we expect that distribution will go nationwide during the course of 1997.

Working Woodlands, Devon and Cornwall

Working Woodlands aims to develop jobs and income from the neglected resources of the many small, semi-natural woodlands scattered through Devon and Cornwall. A partnership of private business, local and national Government, voluntary sector and the European Union will supply the resources and skills needed by some 100 woodland owners and rural businesses. More than 550 people will receive vocational training in a programme which will bring together a wide variety of woodland based enterprise. Building on preliminary market research, which was completed in August 1996, the initiative is expected to contribute £4 million to the local economy, sustaining over 200 jobs.

Woodland Management

Good management of woodland brings both economic and environmental benefits, yet many broadleaf woodlands are not managed. A recent review[13] of the operation of regional woodland initiatives made a number of recommendations on good management, and also highlighted the need to improve co-ordination to maximise their impact. In conjunction with the Forestry Authority and the countryside agencies, we are considering the role that the National Small Woods Association might play in following up this work, and will announce next steps by the end of 1996.

The new Woodland Improvement Grant (WIG), which was launched in 1994, supports a series of targeted projects aimed at high levels of public benefit. By 31 March 1996, 184 hectares of woodland had benefited from the scheme, the first project of which was targeted to the provision of better public access to existing woodlands. In April 1996, we announced two further projects, aimed at improving undermanaged woods and woodland biodiversity. These projects will enable a range of woodland work to be undertaken over the next few years.

East Sussex Woodland Enterprise Centre

In November 1995, the East Sussex Woodland Enterprise Centre won £1 million from Rural Challenge. This will lever in a further £2.2 million of matching funding. The project will involve the development of a new saw mill on a derelict site, training in woodland management, and the development of a community centre. These measures will help bring the predominantly broadleaved woodland in the area back into active management.

Woodland Enterprise Centre, Flimwell

TOURISM

Tourism brings many benefits to the countryside. Not only does it create much needed jobs, but the increased demand it creates for local services, such as shops and transport, can benefit communities where they would otherwise not be viable. However, tourism needs to develop in a way which draws on the character of the countryside and does not destroy the environment on which its popularity depends.

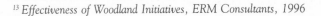

[13] *Effectiveness of Woodland Initiatives, ERM Consultants, 1996*

Impact of Tourism on Rural Settlements

The Rural Development Commission's estimates show that in 1994 tourism was worth at least £9 billion a year to England's rural areas. This represents a substantial proportion of tourism's total contribution to the national economy, which was estimated to be £37 billion, or 5% of GDP.

Tourism has a particularly high potential to create jobs because it is labour intensive. Over 10% of all jobs in Rural Development Areas are in hotels and restaurants alone, and between December 1994 and December 1995, four out of every 10 new jobs in Great Britain were in tourism related occupations. The Commission estimates that there are approaching 400,000 tourism related jobs in rural England, out of the total tourism workforce of 1.5 million.

In March 1996, the Commission published a report[14] on the impact of tourism on rural settlements, which found that:

● the positive contribution made by tourism can go unrecognised because negative impacts such as traffic congestion, are sometimes more visible; and

● the link between tourism and a wide range of benefits such as an increase in the range and viability of shops, businesses and local services is often overlooked.

The report encourages involvement of local communities as a way of maximising potential benefits from tourism and addressing the negative views among residents. Follow up work by the Commission will include guidance on encouraging community involvement as a way of addressing these concerns.

Assistance for Tourism

Rural tourism businesses are generally small and the industry is fragmented. In March 1995 the Department of National Heritage (DNH) published *Tourism: Competing with the Best*, which set out a programme of action, developed in consultation with the industry and tourist boards, to improve international competitiveness, and especially to help smaller independent tourist accommodation business to enhance their performance. We have since taken further action to build on this programme.

In March 1996, following a benchmarking study of 70 small hotels in England, DNH provided 50,000 copies of a good practice guide and self-assessment test[15] to operators of hotels, guest houses and bed and breakfasts. The test allows operators to compare their own performance with the industry standard, and to identify ways of improving it. In partnership with national and local trade associations, local authorities and other bodies, we are working to disseminate this advice and consider what further assistance is needed.

The next phase of *Competing with the Best* includes a review of how the industry uses its main resource - its people. During the autumn of 1996, DNH will publish a report of the review and discuss the findings with the Secretary of State for National Heritage's group of industry advisers, with a view to drawing up a joint action plan to tackle problems such as recruitment difficulties, skill shortages, high staff turnover, and lack of career development.

[14] *The Impact of Tourism on Rural Settlements, RDC*
[15] *Benchmarking for Small Hotels, DNH*

Recognising that rural tourism is an important growth area, DNH and the English Tourist Board (ETB) have jointly commissioned a study of the domestic holiday market in order to identify future opportunities for expansion. The study will recommend ways in which ETB can most effectively intervene to increase the value of domestic tourism. Initial findings will be available in autumn 1996.

Improving Accommodation in the South West

In order to promote tourism throughout the South West Objective 5b area, a package of business support, marketing and capital grants to upgrade facilities will be provided by the West Country Tourist Board. 350 new jobs will be created and a further 250 jobs safeguarded. The total cost of the project, approved in June 1996, is £3.85 million, of which over £1.5 million has been contributed by Challenge for Agriculture.

Sustainable Rural Tourism

Rural tourism goes to the heart of sustainable development because it requires such a sensitive balance to be struck between the needs of the visitor, the character of the local environment and the quality of life of the local community. In November 1995, in order to develop and disseminate principles and good practice for sustainable rural tourism, the Countryside Commission published *Sustainable Rural Tourism - Opportunities for Local Action*, drawing on an evaluation of 21 local tourism initiatives. The report shows how sustainable tourism can be put into practice by the tourism industry, by local communities and by visitors. The report contains a series of case studies which illustrate local achievements.

In March 1996, the Rural Development Commission, with the backing of the ETB and British Airways, published the *Green Audit Kit* which provides practical guidance for tourist businesses. The Kit contains a selection of tried and tested ideas for helping tourism businesses to operate in environmentally friendly ways which also save money.

Market Towns

Small market towns provide important services and employment for rural areas, and their survival is essential for the vitality of surrounding villages. However, many market towns are threatened by changes in the traditional patterns of agricultural production and marketing, coupled with the concentration of some services in larger towns and the growth in out-of-town superstores.

The Rural Development Commission is taking steps to rejuvenate the hearts of small towns which, even in otherwise prosperous areas, can be dismal and uninspiring. The Commission aims to establish a Forum for market towns by the end of 1996. The Forum will be aimed primarily at small rural towns (populations of up to 15,000) and will provide a national network of advice and mutual support. The Forum will disseminate information in the form of advisory notes, provide a support network for practitioners and identify issues of common concern.

To encourage local shopping, in March 1996, Leominster introduced a loyalty scheme. Nearly 100 town centre shops offer discounts for both residents and visitors.

The Commission will also:

● sponsor a national event in 1997 for representatives of small towns to gather best practice;

● support practical research to analyse some of the problems commonly faced by small rural towns; and

● draw together and disseminate case studies showing imaginative responses.

In a related project to help maintain and support these important rural centres. **Business in the Community is co-ordinating a Better Towns competition. The scheme, which is sponsored by BT and the Post Office, will be available to small towns in Cumbria, Leicestershire and Somerset in the autumn of 1996.** The aim is to stimulate a sense of civic responsibility and pride, in order to identify and support initiatives which will contribute towards the revitalisation of small towns. If successful, the programme may be extended to other counties.

Fishing

Our fishermen, and those of other European countries, are affected by the over exploitation of fish stocks. Action to conserve these is essential for the long term sustainability of both the stocks and the industry.

In 1995, we established a Review Group to consider options for improving the Common Fisheries Policy. The Group, which included people with expertise in fishing, environmental and fisheries science, economics and marketing, completed its work in July 1996. Their main conclusions are:

● the biggest problem is the imbalance between fishing capacity and stocks;

● it is not realistic for the United Kingdom to seek to leave the Common Fisheries Policy-changes should be secured from within as a matter of priority;

● quota hopping should be resolved by the Inter-Governmental Conference;

● improvements to the technical conservation measures are required;

● adjustments to the Common Fisheries Policy, including industrial fishing, must be based on sound science; and

● the United Kingdom should press to retain relative stability and the restrictions on access to coastal and other areas in the review to take place in 2002.

The Government welcomed the Group's report[16], and **we will consult on its recommendations.**

[16] *A Review of the Common Fisheries Policy, prepared for UK Fisheries Ministers by the CFP Review Group,* MAFF

In addition to support for fisheries dependent areas available under the Single Regeneration Budget, Rural Challenge and European Structural Funds (such as Objective 2 and 5 programmes), a new European Union initiative, known as PESCA, was launched in England in February 1996. This provides funding to assist the restructuring of the fisheries sector and encourage diversification of economic activity in areas that are heavily dependent on fishing. In England, 25 major ports (and surrounding areas) are eligible, and over £15 million is likely to be available for projects approved up to 1999. Local working groups, including regional partners and local fisheries organisations, have been established to determine local strategies and priorities, and the first grant - £48,000 for the retraining of 20 fishermen in Yorkshire for work in off-shore industries - was approved in July 1996. Other projects under consideration include the development of port facilities, and diversification into non-fishing activities, such as tourism.

Defence

Rural England set out our commitment to using redundant Ministry of Defence (MOD) land for economic regeneration and the creation of employment opportunities. In September 1996, in support of this objective, the MOD and Government Offices agreed guidelines for closer joint working. The new arrangements will ensure that decisions on disposal of sites take account of policies for regeneration and land use, including the need to protect the environment, the needs of local communities and the types of uses which will be attractive to developers.

In autumn 1996, the Rural Development Commission will publish a study on the local impacts of military base and defence industry closures.

Rural Development Commission/Jon Cole-Morgan

Dinton Business Park opened in March 1996 on the site of RAF Chilmark in Wiltshire. 20 small business units have been provided by a partnership between the local authorities, the Rural Development Commission and the European Union's KONVER programme.

3. LIVING IN THE COUNTRYSIDE

Many of us still see the English countryside as an idyllic place, and the attractions are such that the rural population has been growing rapidly. This trend reflects a popular aspiration for a home in the countryside and is an indication of the quality of life which the countryside is perceived to offer. Nevertheless the beauty of the countryside conceals some real problems. The future prosperity of our countryside and of the people who live and work there depends not only on policies being in place to protect it and to stimulate enterprise but also in having thriving communities with reasonable access to essential services. *Rural England* defined our objectives as:

- fostering living rural communities with a mixture of age groups and economic activities;

- reversing the general decline in rural services so that people have reasonable access to the service they need, regardless of where they live;

- improving the performance of public services, making them more responsive to the needs of rural people;

- helping communities to strengthen their public and voluntary institutions so that they can meet their own needs; and

- promoting innovative and cost-effective ways of meeting everyday needs of rural communities.

Population Changes in Rural and Urban Areas 1971-95				('000s)
	1971	1991	1995	1971-1995 % change
Total England	46,412	48,208	48,903	+5.4%
Of which rural	11,071	12,936	13,392	+21.0%
Remainder	35,341	35,272	35,511	+0.5%

Source: Office of National Statistics Mid-Year Population Estimates
Rural is defined as the 150 most rural local authority districts.

SERVICES

Geographic isolation often exacerbates the problems facing rural people especially in remoter areas. This is a particular concern for those who are less mobile or who do not have ready access to a car, the young or elderly, the unemployed or low paid, those with young children, and those who are disabled. In these isolated areas the delivery of services that many of us take for granted in our large towns and cities can be altogether more difficult. The Rural Development Commission 1994 Survey of Rural Services revealed a picture which falls short of the ideal. The Survey will be repeated in 1997.

Chapter One describes our review of the weight to be attached to the sparsity factor in local government finance allocations. However, rural service provision is not wholly a matter of funding levels: in part it depends on the attitude of service providers. It can be all too easy for urban based providers to overlook the needs of their rural customers. In November 1995, in order to encourage public service managers and community groups to think through ways of delivering services of the highest possible quality in rural areas, we launched the Rural Services Checklist as part of the Citizen's Charter initiative.

At a seminar in July 1996, hosted by the Citizens Charter Unit, service providers and rural community council representatives confirmed that the Checklist has been popular - over 6,000 copies have been distributed - and that they considered its contents and presentation to be good. It is too early to expect the Checklist by itself to have produced major changes in the provision of services, but there are encouraging signs that organisations are beginning to use it to guide their approach. Participants at the seminar concluded that future work should concentrate on developing better services through local charters and greater involvement of service users, including establishing relevant targets and indicators.

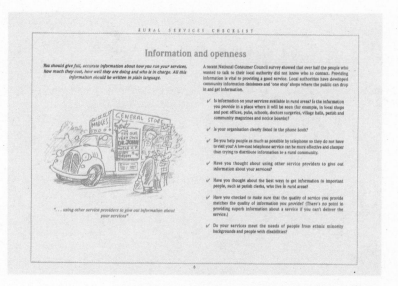

Extract from the Rural Services Checklist

Older people often face particular disadvantage in rural areas because of the difficulty of accessing services at a time of life when they may be especially dependent on them. In February 1996 Help the Aged and the Rural Development Commission published a practical manual[17] describing ways in which cost-effective services can be provided for older people in rural areas. Then in June 1996 the Rural Development Commission and Help the Aged held a national conference following a series of regional seminars to identify the needs of older people in rural communities and how services might be developed to meet them. One of the main problems identified was the difficulty of coordinating services in order to provide them more cost effectively as a way of extending their coverage. Help the Aged therefore intend to establish a national project to encourage service providers to work more closely together. **The Commission will undertake research into the obstacles to joint provision of services by the statutory, voluntary and private sectors and publish the results in mid-1997.**

HOUSING

The maintenance of diverse rural communities is crucial to ensuring a thriving countryside, and we accept the need for a range of housing opportunities in rural areas, particularly for those on low incomes. Our housing policies therefore aim to ensure that:

● local people are not priced out of the housing market; and

● the right size and type of homes are built for those wishing to rent, for first-time buyers and for those with low incomes.

---

[17] *Growing Old in the Countryside: A Case Study Practice Manual,* RDC & Help the Aged

Several measures have been taken to further these aims.

The 1996 Housing Act, which received Royal Assent in July 1996, aims to ensure that people wishing to rent, as well as those wishing to own their own homes, are given a wider choice and a better quality of life. The key measures in the Act are to:

● give housing association tenants the right to buy their homes at a discount under the Purchase Grant scheme, recycling receipts from sales to invest in new housing;

● ensure fairer treatment of people waiting for social housing while retaining the safety net for homeless families and vulnerable people;

● give council tenants the opportunity to vote for new types of social landlord who can bring in private money to improve their estates;

● encourage owners of empty property to let it;

● protect leaseholder home owners against unscrupulous landlords;

● provide speedier action against nuisance neighbours.

Formally opened on 12 October 1995, a new development of 8 houses for local families by Wyvern Rural Housing Association in Pilton, Somerset as part of the Housing Corporation's rural programme targeted at villages with a population of 3,000 or less. The village is one exempt from the Purchase Grant scheme as announced in *Rural England.*

All these measures apply to those living in the countryside as much as to those in our towns and cities. However, in recognition of the special needs of rural areas, and following consultation with rural groups, local authorities, housing associations and others, we decided to exclude small rural settlements in England with a population of 3,000 or fewer from the Purchase Grant scheme. This will help to ensure that there is continued provision of a sufficient number of affordable homes for local people in the countryside in areas where buying or building replacement homes may be difficult.

We have consulted[18] on the specific areas to be included in the exemption. Once an exemption has been put in place we expect it to remain in being for some time: it can only be removed therefore with Parliament's approval, and following consultation with the relevant local authority and bodies representative of registered social landlords. We recognise that in certain cases settlements of more than 3,000 population may face problems in finding replacement property to buy on the open market or sites on which to build new homes. We are willing to consider exempting such settlements where a strong case is made.

In order to give further encouragement to the provision of affordable housing the Housing Corporation introduced a new rural housing enhancement factor in April 1996. This will help rural communities by acknowledging the additional costs that small rural housing associations may face in developing schemes in settlements of 3,000 people or less. The enhancement factor will increase the proportion of Government subsidy which schemes would receive by up to a quarter.

[18] *Consultation Paper on Proposed Rural Exemptions from the Purchase Grant Scheme for Housing Association Tenants, DOE, March 1996*

Local authorities have a key role in ensuring the provision of affordable housing within their area. They are required to draw up housing strategies which determine their priorities and guide the distribution of resources from the Housing Corporation. We are encouraging local authorities with significant rural populations to develop specific rural housing policies as part of their housing strategies. A new Guidance Note published in April 1996[19] drew local authorities' attention, for the first time, to the need to develop these policies. In an accompanying questionnaire we also requested information on rural housing strategies from councils with significant rural populations. The Government Offices will use this information when assessing local authorities' efficiency and effectiveness in meeting local housing needs. In addition, in 1997 we will revise the Housing Strategies booklet which guides local authorities on the development of a strategy and will ensure that it fully covers rural housing needs.

Devon Regional Development Unit

Young people often find it particularly difficult to find affordable housing in rural areas. In April 1996 Centrepoint, a voluntary organisation for young homeless people, began a 3 year demonstration project based in Devon with 50% funding by the Rural Development Commission. This aims to improve the housing options of young people, particularly those who are homeless and vulnerable, by improving inter-agency

working and maximising the use of existing resources. Consultation with district councils, education and health authorities, businesses, church groups and youth agencies will help devise a strategy which will then be developed though a series of new projects such as improving the support provided by the various agencies for young people and increasing the supply of accommodation through the public and private sector.

Rural Housing Schemes can take time to work up and develop. Following a successful pilot project the Rural Development Commission introduced a scheme in June 1996 to assist the appointment of independent individuals as Rural Housing Enablers. The role and operational area of individual enablers will reflect local needs and circumstances. They will work closely with local authorities, housing associations, local communities, landowners, developers and other partners.

Private Rented Sector

In November 1995[20] the Centre for Housing Policy at the University of York completed a study of private renting in rural areas. It was funded by the Joseph Rowntree Foundation and based on an analysis of existing data and a survey of members of the Country Landowners Association (CLA). We will consider the report carefully in relation to our policies aimed at encouraging the private rented sector.

Rural England proposed that the Housing Corporation should include in their Private Rented Sector Relations Programme the objective of supporting initiatives which will expand the involvement of housing associations in the private rented sector in rural areas, with a particular emphasis on bringing back into use long term empty properties. This programme will spend some £0.85 million in 1996/97 and £0.30 million in subsequent years.

---

[19] *The Housing Investment Programme 1996: Guidance Note, DOE*
[20] *Private Renting in Rural Areas, Joseph Rowntree Foundation*

Kennet Farm Cottage Scheme

The Kennet Farm Cottage Scheme, which aims to increase housing opportunities in rural Wiltshire now provides more than 140 dwellings in locations where housing association accommodation is not usually available. Kennet District Council, in partnership with Sarsen Housing Association, identifies empty dwellings and encourages private owners to make available surplus accommodation for rent to Council nominees. The scheme initially focused on farm-based accommodation but now covers a wider range of properties throughout the district. The houses remain in private ownership and, in exchange for a minimum 12 month tenancy, Sarsen guarantees re-housing of the tenant at the end of the term.

In November 1995, this scheme started to identify and buy properties in areas of local housing need. The aim is to increase the stock of affordable rented accommodation in the rural area without involving new building. Kennet/Sarsen's current target is to bring 25 dwellings into the scheme each year.

Making the Best Use of Existing Housing

Rural England recognised the importance of making good use of existing homes which are empty. One way in which we are encouraging this is through the re-use of vacant Ministry of Defence (MOD) homes. The MOD has exceeded its target of disposing of 4,000 surplus properties by summer 1996. The MOD now aims, with the sale of some of the family quarters estate, to raise this total to 5,500 disposals by March 1997.

Energy Efficiency

The energy efficiency of the rural housing stock is less satisfactory than in urban areas. We have therefore taken two further steps to review the effectiveness of our energy efficiency campaigns. During the second quarter of 1996, we undertook research into people's perceptions of energy efficiency and we are now considering the results, including whether there are particular rural issues which need to be addressed.

Two pilot projects in rural areas were launched in spring 1996 under the "Going for Green" campaign. This is promoting the Green Code - a list of actions which individuals can take and which include saving energy and natural resources. Local authorities, in partnership with the voluntary sector will seek to involve whole communities in putting the Green Code into practice.

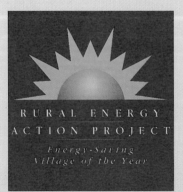

Energy Conscious Village

The Energy Conscious Village of the Year competition formed part of the Oxfordshire Energy Advice Centre's Rural Energy Action Project 1995. It aimed to improve energy efficiency in rural areas of Oxfordshire. Participating communities were encouraged to complete as many home energy surveys as possible with individual homes scoring points by installing energy saving measures, attending energy-saving workshops and by using energy in their homes as efficiently as possible. The winning village for 1995 was Launton near Bicester. The village beat 43 other entries by saving a potential of £25,000 in energy costs and about 350 tonnes of carbon dioxide per year from entering the environment. In February 1996 Dr David Bellamy presented the village with a cheque for £6,000, to help improve the energy efficiency of its community buildings. The competition prompted villages to adopt measures which together saved £132,000 in energy costs and 1,500 tonnes of carbon dioxide. More than 2,650 households took part.

TRANSPORT

For most people living in remoter rural areas, car ownership is more a necessity than a luxury. However, there will continue to be many who do not have a car or do not have access to one when they need it. For them public transport is vital. In other areas such as beauty spots or areas close to urban centres traffic levels pose significant environmental or congestion problems. Here it is becoming increasingly important to develop attractive alternatives to car use.

In April 1996, we published a Green Paper entitled *Transport: The Way Forward*, which was the Government's response to the transport debate launched by the Secretary of State for Transport in 1995. Key themes which emerged in the national debate, and which we intend to pursue, include:

- better planning of transport infrastructure;

- making more efficient use of existing infrastructure;

- reducing dependence on car use, including some additional powers for local authorities to manage traffic;

- switching the emphasis in spending from roads to public transport, cycling and walking; and

- reducing the impact of road freight.

The Government's response includes measures to develop these themes, which will depend on partnership between national and local government, the private sector and individuals. It recognises the distinctive concerns of different rural areas and contains a chapter dedicated to them.

Transport Planning

Local authorities are well placed to ensure that transport policies are responsive to local priorities. In addressing the needs of all road users, they may need to decide on the relative importance of different roads, consider how they should be designed and determine whether priority should be given to public transport. They should also consider how the needs of vulnerable road users such as pedestrians and cyclists should be met. In October 1995 we published *PPG13: A Guide to Better Practice* which shows how local authorities can encourage developments which make more imaginative and efficient use of public transport.

Resources for local transport infrastructure are allocated where the need is greatest using the package approach to funding. This encourages each local authority to produce a transport strategy for its area. Although this approach has so far put proportionately more funds into urban areas than rural ones, we are keen to see package bids for rural locations.

Surrey County Council

The school project aims to reduce the number of journeys made to school by car.

Surrey's Strategic Traffic Plan

Surrey's proximity to London means that pressure from major transport infrastructure such as motorways, railways and international airports is generally a greater concern than the scarcity of public transport which is a problem in remoter parts of the countryside. The County Council therefore introduced STAR - Strategic Action in Rural Areas - in collaboration with the Countryside Commission in March 1996. This scheme will consider the impact of traffic on the quality of the Surrey countryside and try to identify ways of managing traffic better. STAR is made up of five projects which, although individually diverse, form a cohesive whole addressing and implementing the objectives of the overall strategy.

The Surrey Cycleway: is a signed cycleway around rural Surrey, allowing easy access to the countryside, which also warns motorists to expect cyclists in the area;

The Dorking Box: covers 50 square miles and aims to reduce traffic speed and improve conditions for vulnerable road users;

Shere project: aims to improve the quality of life for residents and visitors by reducing congestion and increasing public transport provision to and from the area;

Waveley project: covers about 20 square miles and aims to establish an area for quiet recreational purposes, giving more priority to pedestrians, cyclists and equestrians;

School project: aims to reduce the number of journeys made to school by car.

Buses and Railways

Keeping Purbeck Special

In Purbeck, Dorset, drivers are being encouraged to let the train take the strain following the official opening, in February 1996, of a park-and-ride scheme with a difference. A free staffed car park north of Corfe Castle village means that visitors can now leave their cars there and travel to the Castle and Swanage by steam train. The scheme is a pilot project to alleviate traffic congestion and parking problems in Corfe Castle and is the first step in an integrated transport programme which will allow 4.5 million visitors per year to move around Purbeck without harming the environment.

Other measures include extending the railway to Wareham, a seasonal ferry between Bournemouth and Swanage, cycle hire and innovative use of signing and access restrictions. The project is an example of the work of the Purbeck Heritage Committee which brings together conservation and tourism interests with landowners and local authorities and is part of a strategy of "Keeping Purbeck Special".

Whilst most rural public transport involves buses, railways provide an important service in some areas. We will therefore continue to make subsidy available for those rural rail services franchised as part of the privatisation of British Rail and specified in the Passenger Service Requirement (PSR) for each franchise. These set out a core level of services which each franchise is obliged to run. PSRs take the existing British Rail timetable as their starting point and are agreed following consultation with appropriate local authorities and Rail Users' Consultative

Committees. In this way vulnerable services, which are often in rural areas, are protected whilst giving operators flexibility to tailor their services to respond to the market. All franchisees to date are providing services over and above the PSR.

PSRs published in summer 1996 have protected rural services in East Anglia, Cornwall and between Hereford and Shrewsbury. Consultation in these regions has led to the further safeguarding of services provided in the early morning, late evening and on Sundays, connections with InterCity and ferry services and services which stop at more intermediate stations.

Catch the Bus to Take the Train

In February 1996, the first rail franchise South West Trains (run by the bus operating group Stagecoach Holdings PLC) announced the introduction of two bus links between Romsey and Winchester and Borden and Liphook to connect with South West Trains main line services. Borden in Hampshire does not have a railway station and has a very infrequent bus service to Liphook, the nearest main line railhead. The bus will have a large luggage pen and train tickets can be bought on the bus. Signs in the station and key bus stops will be upgraded to include Rail-Link information and there will be a radio link between the bus and Liphook rail station.

Community and Voluntary Transport

In sparsely populated parts of the countryside solutions to transport needs often involve flexible and innovative approaches, targeted on local circumstances and drawing on the resources of the community. We provide support for community transport in the countryside in part through the Rural Transport Development Fund which is administered by the Rural Development Commission. In May 1996 we widened the scope of the Fund and made it more flexible. We have also increased our support for the Fund in 1996/97 by over 40% to £1.25 million. In addition to supporting transport schemes which are available to the general public, the Fund can now also be used to support:

- schemes for particular groups of people such as elderly, disabled and young people;
- the cost of converting community buses to allow people with disabilities to use them;
- the provision of waiting points and bus shelters; and
- posts to enable public sector or charitable organisations to develop rural services.

The Commission expects to be able to support up to 80 new projects a year as well as 6 to 8 posts in local authorities and other organisations.

Parish councils are well placed to develop solutions to local community transport needs. *Rural England* therefore consulted on proposals for extending their powers and we intend to introduce legislation at the earliest possible opportunity. Our detailed proposals would allow parishes to:

- conduct surveys on transport needs;
- support community transport schemes including the training of volunteers and staff and the marketing of services;
- pay for taxis to transport needy residents;
- organise car sharing schemes;
- collect and disseminate passenger transport information;
- fund traffic calming measures.

Community groups and volunteers who are running transport schemes may need support and guidance. In June 1996 the Rural Development Commission approved a three year project, in conjunction with the Community Transport Association. This will help rural communities, including parish councils, to assess their transport needs and define solutions, and will provide training materials for volunteers involved in local transport schemes. In March 1996 the Commission published a good practice guide to rural transport schemes[21] which it distributed widely, including to all rural parish councils.

Postbuses

One creative response to local transport needs has been the use of Postbuses. During 1996 the Royal Mail introduced seven dedicated Divisional Postbus Development Managers with responsibility for developing and implementing new routes. They will work with local authorities, the Rural Development Commission and other interested organisations to identify and establish new routes. Since October 1995, Postbus routes have opened in Thetford and Hexham and new routes are under consideration in the North East at Alnwick, Seahouses and Bamburgh and in Dorchester in the South West. The Royal Mail remains committed to its aim to establish 20 new routes a year until 1999.

Cycling

We believe that cycling should be an integral part of a sustainable transport policy. At a national conference in July 1996, we launched the National Cycling Strategy, drawn up by a Steering Group comprising representatives of Government Departments, local authorities, commercial interests and voluntary organisations. The Strategy aims to stimulate an increase in the use of cycles, through the development of good practice and improved facilities for cyclists. A key objective of the Strategy is to provide wider access for cyclists, including linking urban route networks into the countryside through the National Cycle Network being promoted by Sustrans, and through other recreation and tourism cycle routes.

Countryside Commission

Oxenholme Station

We believe it is realistic to seek to double current levels of cycling by the year 2002 and again by 2012. We have asked local authorities to play their part in improving conditions for cyclists, and invited them to identify how they can contribute to realising the national target.

The Strategy highlights the complementary roles of cycling and public transport, especially trains. The 1995 Cycle Challenge competition is bringing forward a wide variety of innovative ideas to encourage growth in cycle use. Amongst the 62 successful projects are some designed to improve the carriage of bicycles on trains and parking at railway stations. For example, Anglia Railways, in partnership with local authorities, Transport 2000 and the Cyclists' Public Affairs Group, are modifying rolling stock to carry up to six bikes. In addition, local stations will become more cycle friendly with improved access and good cycle parking facilities.

Traffic Calming

Traffic calming, in which engineering and other measures encourage drivers to modify their speeds, can be highly effective at reducing road accidents and traffic flows. However, there has been some concern that the gains made might be at the expense of increased noise and other environmental impact.

[21] *Country Lifelines - Good Practice in Rural Transport, RDC*

Building on the experience of the Village Speed Control Working Group Study in 1994, the Department of Transport (DOT) has initiated monitoring of the effectiveness of calming schemes on trunk roads. A report on the A49 at Craven Arms in Shropshire[22], found that the scheme had been successful, in part at least, in reducing speeds and increasing pedestrian safety; however, the report highlights the difficulty of designing measures which are both effective and acceptable to the community. A report on the A47 at Thorney, Cambridgeshire, will be published in the first half of 1997, and DOT will commission further monitoring of other schemes.

In *Rural England*, we recognised the need for traffic calming measures to be sensitive to their surroundings. In January 1996, DOT published *Traffic Advisory Leaflet 1/96*, on traffic management in historic areas. This emphasises that engineering works should be carried out as part of an integrated approach to the townscape, within a wider traffic management strategy. Other Traffic Advisory Leaflets published in 1996, on road humps, emissions, and vehicle noise, provide further guidance.

It is also important that such measures are based on consultation with local residents. In order to strengthen best practice, both in design and local participation, the Countryside Commission will establish a Countryside Traffic Measures Group. In partnership with DOT and local authorities, the Group will encourage and monitor innovative local schemes, designed with sensitivity to the local environment in particular to provide a safer environment for pedestrians, cyclists and horse riders. We expect the Countryside Commission to invite proposals for pilot projects and establish the Group before the end of 1996.

HEALTH AND SOCIAL CARE

We are committed to improving health and social care across the country and to encouraging flexible delivery in ways which respond best to the needs of rural people. As part of this commitment the Department of Health (DOH) is developing a workbook of good practice for health and social care in rural areas. In June 1996, professionals and individuals from the NHS, local authorities and the voluntary sector took part with the NHS executive in a two-day workshop to consider the purpose and content of the workbook as a collaborative venture. Their discussions were informed by research carried out by the University of Liverpool and the Wessex Institute for Public Health into new developments in rural health services and social care. The workbook, which will describe new developments in services and innovative practice being developed by organisations and individuals in rural areas for local people, will be published in December 1996.

Primary Care

In October 1995 DOH launched a debate on the ways in which the services provided by family doctors and other primary care professionals such as nurses, pharmacists and optometrists should develop in the next 5 to 10 years. The report *Primary Care: the Future*, which DOH published in June 1996, reflects the balance and range of responses. It identifies principles which will guide the future development of primary care and seven possible areas for national and local action to underpin them. A wide range of ideas were put forward, making clear the importance of diverse approaches within a national health service with a set of coherent objectives and services. Local solutions to local problems was a key message, recognising that different solutions are needed for the problems of rural areas to those in urban and suburban areas. Following further consultation to reach an understanding of the best way to develop these ideas, we are working to identify the practical steps, including possible legislation, we should take to put these ideas into practice. We will announce our conclusion in the autumn.

---

[22] *Transport Research Laboratory, August 1996.*

Community Nursing

A nurse prescribing pilot scheme, involving around 60 nurses, half from rural or semi rural practices, began in 1994. Nurse prescribing enables district nurses, health visitors and practice nurses who have obtained the relevant qualification to prescribe from a limited list of dressings, creams and medicines. In April 1996, in order to help measure the effects of nurse prescribing over both fundholding and non-fundholding practices, the scheme was extended to cover a whole district community NHS trust in Lancashire. Over 150 nurses are now participating, linked to some 60 GP practices. **We will decide whether to extend the scheme after a further evaluation.**

Secondary Care

Secondary care, which is provided by hospitals, has been concentrated in towns and cities. However, community hospitals and other small units are increasingly providing a range of health services closer to patients' homes, particularly in rural communities. The Standing Medical and Nursing and Midwifery Advisory Committees issued a joint report in January 1996[23] to help such small units maintain standards while providing a more local service.

Ambulance Services

At present ambulance services are expected to give equal priority to all 999 calls. In all areas ambulance services are expected to reach 50% of calls within eight minutes. In rural areas ambulance services are expected to reach 95% of calls within 19 minutes and in urban areas 95% of calls within 14 minutes. In 1995/96 over 90% of responses to 999 calls to ambulance services met these targets.

In July 1996 DOH published a Report of a Steering Group on the Review of Ambulance Performance Standards. This Report suggested that in the future ambulance services introduce systems allowing them to prioritise calls so that the most serious cases, where life is at risk, which are about 25% of the total, get the fastest response. It is thought that such systems could enable up to 3,000 more lives to be saved in England. Following the review, we have established a common response time for both rural and urban services to reach life-threatening emergencies within eight minutes. Under a new Patient's Charter standard which was published in September 1996, 75% of responses are expected to reach this target by the year 2001.

In sparsely populated areas it may prove difficult to get an ambulance to the scene of an incident within the eight minute target. The Report suggests ways that ambulance services in rural areas can address these problems. "First responder" schemes are one option. Ambulance services would train volunteers in the community to provide basic life support and to use a defibrillator in the event of a cardiac arrest. Ambulance services would be responsible for making arrangements for calling out first responders where necessary.

Health Authorities

The formula which is used to determine the allocation of funds to health authorities for their hospital and community health services is kept under review. It was last reviewed in 1994 to take account of new information and better statistical techniques, and this data informed the 1996/97 allocations.

---

[23] *Maintaining High Quality Care in Smaller Units: A Report of a Joint Working Group of the Standing Medical & Nursing & Midwifery Advisory Committees.*

Whilst there is no evidence to suggest that rurality affects the need for hospital services, it may be a more significant factor in the need for community health services. A team from the Universities of Plymouth and Kent has been commissioned to investigate the need associated with community health services. **Their report will be published in autumn 1996 and will be taken into account in determining health authorities' funding allocations for 1997/98.**

In addition, DOH is carrying out a fundamental review of the part of the formula related to unavoidable geographical variations in the cost of staff, land and buildings - the market forces factor. This work will also consider if there are other sources of cost variation, including the effect of rurality on the cost of providing community nursing and ambulance services. **We aim to complete this work in time to inform the 1997/98 funding allocations.**

On 1 April 1996 district health authorities and family health service authorities were merged to form health authorities. The creation of a single organisation responsible for all local health services - primary, community and acute (secondary) - enables these services to be coordinated in a way which is much more sensitive to local needs.

Social and Community Care

Community care aims to ensure that vulnerable people receive the support they need to enable them to live as independently as possible in their own homes or communities. It is obviously important for community care to be tailored to individuals' needs and to local circumstances. In September 1995 DOH published guidance on community care plans, which emphasised the importance of addressing the particular needs of rural ideas.

Malmesbury and District Community Transport

Providing a Sustainable Service to Users and Carers in Rural Bedfordshire

In April 1996, the Bedfordshire Rural Community Charity began a new project designed to give targeted support to rural carers and users in their own communities. The Charity aims to establish day centres and village care schemes in rural communities across Bedfordshire and to develop and disseminate self-help packs. The project, which will last for two years, will seek to identify patterns of good practice which may be replicated in other rural areas.

In February 1996 we published guidance on the Carers (Recognition and Services) Act 1995[24] which highlighted issues for rural carers. The Act, which came into force on 1 April, means that carers who provide substantial care on a regular basis are now entitled to an assessment of their ability to provide and continue to provide care. The results of the carer's assessment are taken into account when decisions are made about services for the person for whom care is being provided.

---

[24] *Carers (Recognition and Services) Act 1995: Policy Guidance and Practice Guide, DOH*

EDUCATION

Pre-School Education

Rural Development Commission/A Dench

The availability of nursery education for children under the age of five varies throughout the country, as do standards. By introducing a nursery voucher scheme, we hope that more good quality nursery places will become available to meet parental demand and expectations.

Norfolk, a predominantly rural area, is one of the four areas participating in Phase I of our nursery vouchers scheme which was introduced in April 1996. Preliminary research on the scheme by the Pre-school Learning Alliance, an educational charity, estimated that only 280 children in Norfolk previously received any fee subsidies, whereas over 95% of parents have

Old School House
Day Nursery,
Stetchworth, Suffolk

now applied for vouchers and made use of them. The scheme has enabled existing providers to expand. In evaluating the scheme we will pay close attention to its impact in a rural county. **The evaluation will inform Phase II of the scheme which we will introduce in April 1997.**

Rural Schools

Rural schools remain a valuable resource, not only for the education they provide for local children, but also for the focus they provide for the community they serve, the sense of security they bring to the children, and the balance they give to village life.

The number of closures of small village schools has been of concern to many people. The Secretary of State for Education whilst pressing education authorities to be cost effective:

- will not normally approve the closure of a school where the alternative schooling on offer is not of at least equivalent quality;

- weighs very carefully the consequences of closure proposals, including for example, the impact on the children's journey to school, as well as the effect on the wider community;

- accepts the need to preserve accessibility of schooling for young children as a justification for retaining surplus places.

Self Government for Schools

The White Paper *Self Government for Schools*, published in June 1996, proposes new measures to extend self government for all schools, including those serving rural communities, by giving them more power to decide how to spend their budgets, and by giving grant-maintained schools new freedoms to decide how they should develop. It proposes new ways of extending choice and diversity, by encouraging new grammar schools, by giving all schools more power to select pupils by ability or aptitude, and by helping more schools to specialise in particular subjects.

New Technology

Technological advances have enormous potential for education, particularly in sparsely populated areas. During 1995 we therefore consulted with the education service and telecommunications industry on the contribution that new technologies can make to lifelong learning. In November 1995 we published our conclusions in *Superhighways for Education: The*

Way Forward. We announced a new £10 million programme of 23 projects which will pilot medium and high speed networking technologies in all sectors of education, including rural schools. **We will publish the results of these projects in Spring 1997**.

Benefits Agency Video Link in the West Country

The Benefits Agency have been looking at ways to improve services to rural areas, and in conjunction with Devon County Council have established a trial video link between the Citizens Advice Bureau in Okehampton and the Benefits Agency office in Exeter. The project, which reduces the need for time consuming and expensive journeys to Exeter, went live in August 1996; if successful, it will be extended more widely within the region.

Sports Facilities

Those who live in the countryside often have limited access to sports facilities. It is therefore important to make the best possible use of those facilities which are available such as school playing fields. In November 1995, the Department for Education and Employment published a booklet *Our School - Your School* which encourages schools to make their premises available to the community. It stresses the special position of schools in rural areas.

In January 1996, the Sports Council announced a change to its grants from the Lottery Sports Fund to provide up to 90% of the cost of new or refurbished sports facilities in priority areas, including all of the Rural Development Areas. The emphasis is on providing maximum community benefit - for example, clubs submitting applications will be expected to increase their membership, and school premises must be readily available for wider community use.

SHOPS AND POST OFFICES

The small general store or post office provides a focal point in many small villages and can be a lifeline for some members of the community. The demise of a village shop can be a particularly severe blow to the community. We have taken a number of measures which recognise the particular problems facing these businesses.

Business Rates

Research shows that business rates impose a more substantial burden on the smallest businesses, especially small shops. Therefore with the help of individuals and organisations such as the Rural Development Commission and the Village Retail Services Association (ViRSA), we drew up proposals to provide rate relief for village general stores and post offices, and published them for consultation[25] in May 1996. The proposals involve:

- A mandatory scheme which would give 50% rate relief to all general stores and post offices with rateable values of less than £5,000 which are the only such outlets in rural settlements of less than 3,000 people.

- A discretionary scheme under which local authorities would be able to top-up the mandatory relief to 100% and to give up to 100% relief to other shops, post offices and businesses such as pubs in the same settlements if they are of benefit to the community.

---

[25] *Rate Relief for Village Shops, A consultation paper linked to the Rural White Paper: "Rural England", DOE*

The Exchequer will meet the full costs of the mandatory scheme and 75% of the cost of any discretionary relief. The consultation period closed on 14 June 1996. **We are considering the results of the consultation and will introduce legislation at the earliest opportunity.**

 We also intend to retain the power of local authorities to give hardship relief. Since the ways in which local authorities operate this scheme vary greatly, **we will issue fresh guidance by the end of 1996.** This will identify good practice and emphasise the importance of authorities having clear and widely understood policies and explaining the reasons for the decisions they reach.

Ensuring Survival

Easing the financial burden on shopkeepers is only one way of ensuring their survival. We encourage local authorities, communities themselves and others to look for new and innovative ways of supporting businesses within their locality.

VILLAGE SHOP
Support Scheme

Norfolk Village Shops Initiative

South Norfolk District Council, Norfolk and Waveney TEC, the Rural Development Commission and Tesco have teamed up to pilot a scheme aimed at helping village stores survive. The scheme, launched in June 1996, will run for two years and will help 24 shop owners in South Norfolk District re-examine their businesses, offering funding and training to help them remain viable.

 Between October and December 1995 the Rural Development Commission piloted a grant scheme in Gloucestershire and West Sussex. The scheme helped shops in smaller rural communities by providing 50% of the costs of work which had been identified by the shopkeeper and the Commission's retail consultant as part of a plan to improve the shop's commercial viability. Work included investment in improving and modernising the shop and equipment as well as training and marketing. For example, one store diversified its business through the installation of an in-store bakery; another installed an electronic point of sales scanning system to improve stock management; and a third provided a car park to give better access to the shop. The Commission has decided to extend the scheme to areas where other organisations are prepared to work in partnership with the Commission by providing funding and helping with the management of the scheme.

 During 1996, the Rural Development Commission and ViRSA have clarified their respective roles to ensure that they are complementary. The Commission will concentrate on assisting shopkeepers whereas ViRSA will support communities which wish to take action to save their local shop. Their work at local level will take account of the activity of other local organisations such as Rural Community Councils, local authorities, and TECs.

The Bull Mini Store

In August 1995 the post office and village store in East Farleigh in Kent were closed. A public meeting was organised by East Farleigh Parish Council at which the Rural Development Commission's Retail Advisor and a Post Office representative recommended a community shop. Villagers pooled their efforts and resources under a project steering committee, and the new shop and post office reopened in June 1996 in a portable cabin in the car park of the village pub. Villagers raised money, and grants were received from the Parish Council, Kent Rural Community Council and the Rural Development Commission. Help and advice were given by Nurdin & Peacock Cash & Carry and ViRSA. The East Farleigh Village Shop Association Ltd., which is made up of villagers, now runs the shop seven days a week and aims to stock meat, fish and cheese from local traders. A request book invites customers to ask for other goods to be stocked.

East Farleigh Village Shop Association Ltd

Post Offices

We remain committed to a nationwide network of post offices. The Post Office has a network of 19,400 offices nationwide, about half of which are in rural areas. Post offices provide a wide range of services which are particularly valuable in rural areas. Post Office Counters Limited's (POCL) objective is that there should be no net post office closures. Disappointingly, in 1995/96 there was a net reduction of 193 offices compared with an average annual net reduction of 175 over the previous four years. Virtually all these closures were the result of there being no suitable candidate to continue running the office once the existing subpostmaster had retired or left. POCL is therefore continuing to encourage people to run local services by supporting the use of community post offices and is developing new ways of supporting subpostmasters.

In June 1996 POCL developed a "Counters Club" scheme with Palmer & Harvey McLean which is designed to help all independent subpostmasters. The scheme brings together subpostmasters to give them the buying power of a multiple group and the facility to have deliveries made to their post office stores. The scheme also provides subpostmasters with retail advice to help them improve their businesses.

In order to improve the viability of post offices we have allowed POCL greater freedom to offer new services. POCL is now the most extensive *bureau de change* chain and the largest retail outlet for the National Lottery, and travel insurance is now available from virtually all post offices. The progressive introduction of automation and benefits payments cards from autumn 1996 will facilitate the provision of a more secure, efficient and economic service to post office customers. Automation will also assist with the development and delivery of new products.

National Lottery

The National Lottery provides an unprececented opportunity for communities in all parts of the country, including rural areas, to carry forward the sort of projects that would previously have been beyond their reach. Funds are available for sport, arts, heritage, charities and events to mark the Millennium. By the end of September 1996, the Lottery had raised over £2.4 billion for good causes and the eleven distributing bodies had made 9,849 awards totalling £2.09 billion to projects of all sizes in all parts of the United Kingdom.

Although it is not yet possible to say exactly how much funding has gone to rural areas, there is some evidence that they are not doing as well as cities and urban areas. **We will consider the extent of this problem and in the meantime encourage those in rural areas to put together applications for Lottery funds and thus ensure that they receive the maximum possible benefit from this new source of funds.**

CRIME AND POLICING

Since 1992 there has been an 8 per cent fall in recorded crimes in non-metropolitan forces. There were 250,000 fewer crimes in 1995 than in 1992. In 1995 recorded crime fell by 3 per cent nationally compared with 1994, with a 3.5 per cent fall recorded by non-metropolitan forces. Close examination of forces' figures shows.that there are few trends emerging in 1995 that distinguish the more rural forces from the more urban ones. The only ones of note are that a one per cent fall in burglary in 1995 was mostly in the more rural of forces; and that some of the largest increases in theft from the person occurred in the more rural of forces.

Crime Prevention

 In 1994, the Rural Development Commission and some local authorities commissioned Crime Concern to carry out four local surveys of young peoples' involvement in, and concerns about, crime. The results of the research, which showed that the involvement of young people in criminal and anti-social activity in rural areas differs little from national trends, were reported at Crime Concern's national conference in June 1996.

 Crime Concern, with the support of the TSB Foundation and the Rural Development Commission, published a guide for parish councils[26] in October 1995. This contained a wealth of case studies giving practical advice on crime prevention and encouraged parish councils to take effective action using their existing powers. Over 6,000 copies have been sold, and it has been discussed at many conferences.

 Rural England proposed extending the powers of parish councils to community policing, to enable them to work more closely with the police by, for example, contributing towards the costs of recruiting, training and equipping local neighbourhood special constables in their area. **We propose to give parish councils these powers in two ways. Firstly by adding parish councils to the list of councils authorised under the Police Act 1996 to make grants to police authorities, and secondly by a new provision which will allow parish and community councils to raise and spend money for crime prevention. Following consultation we are preparing proposals for legislation which we will discuss with the local authority associations and other bodies with a direct interest.**

---

[26] *Cutting Crime in Rural Areas, a Practical Guide for Parish Councils*

East Leicestershire Problem Oriented Policing Pilot

This pilot scheme involves collaboration between Leicestershire Police, Neighbourhood Watch, parish constables, parish councils and the Home Office Police Research Group.

In November 1995, following a re-organisation of Leicestershire Police into parish based neighbourhood policing units, action groups were formed by the Neighbourhood Police Officers in conjunction with parish councils and residents. These identify the main local crime and disorder problems and possible solutions to them. Priority solutions are then used to form the local Policing Plan.

Action plans have included:

- youth diversion programmes, involving youth clubs and drop in centres;

- a residents' visiting programme to address elderly residents' isolation and fear of attack;

- measures to stop the traffic hazard caused by the repeated straying of sheep.

Community Action

We continue to provide support for special constables - members of the community who devote part of their spare time to serving as uniformed police constables with the same powers as regular police officers. The number of specials in England and Wales has remained constant at about 20,000 for the last three years; the target of 30,000 by the end of 1996 proved unrealistic. However, a national recruitment campaign and the provision of a £10 million Special Constabulary Challenge Fund in 1995/96 and 1996/97 should see a substantial increase in numbers by the end of 1997. Recommendations from the Working Group which reviewed the Special Constabulary during 1995/96 should also improve recruitment processes, retention, and training.

The target of 3,000 neighbourhood special constables by the end of 1996 also proved unattainable. There are currently about 1,500 specials deployed on neighbourhood duties, many in rural areas. One of the objectives of the Challenge Fund in 1996/97 is to ensure the most effective use of volunteers' skills and experience in order to help us reach our targets.

Village Constable Scheme in Solihull

West Midlands Police have formed a successful partnership with a number of villages in the rural areas of the Borough of Solihull. With the support of the residents, a "Village Constable" scheme has been developed and there are currently 13 neighbourhood special constables in the team that patrols the villages. There is a continuing campaign to recruit more volunteers: in August 1996 the force took delivery of a multi purpose vehicle to convey the specials around the villages and to use at local events and recruiting displays. The Ford Galaxy People Mover was part sponsored by Ford and funded by a grant from the Special Constabulary Challenge Fund.

Watch Schemes

There are now 153,000 Neighbourhood Watch schemes throughout England and Wales and many examples of more specific watch schemes such as Farm Watch, Horse Watch, and School Watch. In November 1996 the Home Office will issue a new guide for Neighbourhood Watch schemes designed to help them tackle local problems.

Spy-in-the-Sky

A Farm Watch scheme was introduced in the Longdendale Valley, Derbyshire, in September 1995 at the request of the farming community. 43 members are now registered. If an incident such as sheep stealing occurs in the area the details are entered onto the crime prevention advice system "Ring Master". The Farm Watch members automatically receive a warning message by phone.

In February 1996, in response to the theft of a growing number of trailers and other farm equipment throughout the area, the Greater Manchester Police and Derbyshire Constabulary decided to extend the scheme by using the Force's helicopter. Farmers in the valley are encouraged to post-code the tops of their trailers with 16" high, difficult to remove, black vinyl letters printed on a white background which make identification from the sky easier. Farmers are also putting the serial numbers of any smaller farm equipment onto the Farm Watch computer to identify stolen farm machinery.

Greater Manchester Police

CCTV

Closed circuit television (CCTV) surveillance systems are a useful development in crime prevention, helping to reduce levels of crime and make people feel more secure. In November 1995 we announced the second CCTV Challenge Competition, which made over £17 milllion available to support CCTV partnerships. The winners were announced in June 1996. About a quarter of the public area winners were in rural towns or villages. This amounts to around 50 new rural CCTV systems. They included Amesbury in Wiltshire which has been awarded £32,500 to help install a six-camera CCTV system aimed at reducing crime in the town centre. The third CCTV Challenge Competition will make a further £15 million available for CCTV in 1997/98.

Wildlife Crime

In November 1995 we launched the *Partnership for Action Against Wildlife Crime*. Wildlife species are subject to a mass of controls, the enforcement of which has not always been a priority. In more recent years, concern about the misuse and exploitation of wildlife has been growing. Wildlife crime is becoming more organised and better co-ordinated, and the Partnership's main tasks are therefore to provide a forum for better communication and co-ordination between the organisations involved and a strategic overview of law enforcement activity. We announced at the launch that we would:

● issue practical advice on the application of DNA techniques to wildlife crime by the end of 1996;

● sponsor research to establish DNA tests for birds of prey; and

● finance a guide to wildlife enforcement to be published in October 1996 for wildlife enforcement practitioners.

Police and Fire Service Targets

Each police force operates a graded response policy which is defined according to local circumstances and priorities. Police forces are expected to set and publish local targets which reflect local needs and priorities. Most forces have separate targets for their urban and rural areas against which performance is judged and the typical rural target is to respond to incidents requiring an immediate response within 20 minutes.

The Audit Commission's latest annual report[27] found that many forces have shown improvements in performance and that 85% of forces met their targets for 80% of incidents or more compared with 71% in 1993/94.

The fire service also has national recommended standards of cover. In 1994/95, the service met the national recommended response times to fire calls on 95% of occasions compared with 94% in 1993/94. A similar level of achievement applies both to metropolitan and to largely rural fire authority areas.

---

[27] *Local Authority Performance Indicators 1994/95, Vol 3, Police and Fire Services, HMSO*

4. A GREEN AND PLEASANT LAND

The English countryside is a resource for the nation as a whole and most people have far more opportunity to enjoy it than was once the case. However, our landscapes and wildlife are finite assets. The countryside supplies many essential natural resources, but in some areas is under pressure from their exploitation, as well as from intensive farming, development and traffic.

Rural England defined our collective responsibility to:

- conserve the countryside's natural assets, managing them wisely and avoiding irreversible damage wherever possible in order to maintain or enhance their value for generations to come;

- reverse the decline in wildlife, sustaining the wealth of flora and fauna across the countryside and conserving the population of rare species;

- maintain the diversity of rural landscapes;

- redress the environmental damage of the past and ensure that unavoidable damage in the future is offset wherever possible through other environmental improvements;

- safeguard the quality and particular character of rural towns and villages;

- increase opportunities for people to enjoy the countryside for recreation;

- acknowledge and exploit the interdependence of environmental protection and economic development;

- establish processes at national and local level to reconcile competing demands in an open and accessible manner.

It acknowledged that these objectives would be met by a mix of advice, incentives and regulation, and through action by businesses, the public sector, voluntary groups and individuals.

Monitoring and Research

Rural England stressed the importance of basing policies on the best information available about the state of the environment, by monitoring trends in the countryside and improving access to this information.

 The Countryside Survey 1990 provided a baseline against which future changes in countryside features, species and habitats can be measured. In May 1996, a policy review strongly supported the Survey and recommended repeating it at regular intervals. In conjunction with the Natural Environment Research Council (NERC) we have begun work to ensure that Countryside Survey 2000 is as relevant, reliable and cost-effective as possible. We are also conducting a further specific survey on ponds.

In order to improve the integration and accessibility of data on the countryside so that better use can be made of it, DOE has extended the range of data available to users of the Countryside Information System (CIS). The system now includes information on designated areas, wildlife distributions, farm types, land cover and soils. An enhanced version of CIS, with a full catalogue of environmental information, is available.

We also need to improve our understanding of the changes in the countryside and their consequences. We are doing this in a number of ways. For example, a study of the current status and future prospects for key habitats, including lowland heaths, lime-rich grasslands, uplands and the coast, **will be published in autumn 1996.** We have started a major study to help understand the ecological causes of change in the countryside; the three year study, **which will report in 1998,** aims to explain the reasons for change in the botanical diversity of farmland, moorland, hedgerows and roadside verges.

Understanding

We believe it is important that those who live in our towns and cities understand rural issues, including the needs of a working environment which supports the production of our food and other resources. We would like all primary schools to give their pupils an opportunity to visit farms, forest or other countryside features.

Our strategy for environmental education, which was announced in June 1996, will help to foster an understanding of rural as well as urban, national and global issues. We are considering whether to establish a panel to bring together representatives from education, training, and business with environmental specialists to progress work on environmental education. Countryside specialists could have a role to play. **We aim to announce conclusions before the end of 1996.**

Farmlink

Farmlink is a Groundwork partnership project which aims to help children to understand and respect the countryside, and to create beneficial links between farmers and the local urban communities. Each voluntary long-term partnership is between a farmer and a school which makes several visits to the farm each year. Since 1992, with the help of MAFF funding, over 180 links have been set up; the project is being further sponsored until March 1998, with a target of another 180 links to be achieved.

A child from a Barnet primary school visiting College Farm in north west London

Dr Richard Shaw

The Countryside Commission's new strategy *A Living Countryside*, published in March 1996, included a commitment to promote public information and understanding about the countryside. **A framework for developing this work will be completed by the end of 1996.**

Luton and South Bedfordshire Chilterns Initiative

This six year project, which began in April 1996, aims to resolve conflicts and improve the relationship between urban and rural areas, where the Chilterns Area of Outstanding Natural Beauty (AONB) meets the Luton, Dunstable and Houghton Regis conurbation. The area contains nationally important chalk grassland, and is under pressure from people using the area for recreation. A partnership, including local authorities, the Wildlife Trust, English Nature and the Countryside Commission will work with businesses and landowners to conserve and enhance the area, balancing the needs of those who work and live there with those who visit. Objectives include promoting walking, cycling and public transport routes between town and country, countryside education and developing recreational activities in the built-up areas.

Urban Greening

Improving the urban environment is a prerequisite for the protection of rural England. We are therefore committed to enhancing the quality, design, conservation value and community use of open green space in order to make our towns and cities more attractive places in which to live.

The *Greening the City* initiative, launched in October 1995, aims to develop national good practice for urban greening. During 1996 we have arranged a series of seminars to draw together information and experience, supported by an Advisory Group of representatives of local authorities, voluntary organisations, and the private sector. **We will publish the good practice guide in autumn 1996.** We expect to follow the launch with further seminars to provide advice to practitioners, and to encourage the involvement of local communities.

Rural England invited the Countryside Commission, with other agencies, to explore ways of focusing resources on river corridors. **The Countryside Commission will prepare a framework for action in 1997.**

Urban trees are important not only because they enhance our surroundings but also because they can filter pollution and provide shelter and food for wildlife in the city. But space in towns and cities is limited, and often has to be shared. Tree strategies are a useful mechanism to improve the conditions and care of urban trees. In February 1996, in partnership with the Countryside Commission, we published guidelines for London Boroughs on the preparation of trees strategies[28]. The guidelines have wider relevance for all those concerned with protecting and enhancing the benefits which urban trees can offer.

Hedgerows

Hedgerows are a distinctive feature of the English countryside, which sustain many forms of wildlife, as well as providing shelter for crops and livestock. Evidence showed that, although removal was not the problem it had been in the 1980s, important hedgerows remain vulnerable. In order to complement the incentive schemes which encourage landowners to manage hedgerows positively, the Environment Act 1995 provided powers to introduce regulations which would protect important hedgerows.

[28] *Planning for London's Trees, Cobham Resource Consultants*

We will publish draft regulations for public consultation in October 1996. Our proposals would protect important hedgerows by requiring a land manager who wishes to remove a hedgerow to notify the local planning authority before doing so; the local planning authority must refuse consent to the removal if the hedge is considered to be important. The draft regulations incorporate criteria, based on a study by ADAS, which planning authorities must use in determining whether a hedgerow is important for wildlife or is of historic interest.

The draft regulations seek to strike a balance between the concerns of the public to protect hedgerows, and the economic interests of land managers. We intend to lay the new regulations before Parliament by the end of 1996.

Historic Landscapes

It is especially important to protect historic landscape features because once destroyed, whether by built development or agriculture, they cannot be restored. Guidance is provided to local authorities in the Planning Policy Guidance notes. In May 1996, the Department of National Heritage issued a consultation paper[29] seeking views on whether current statutory controls are adequate. Whilst mainly concerned with policy on listed buildings, views were also sought on conservation areas and archaeological sites. We will consider whether any changes are necessary in the light of comments received.

Monuments

There are over 600,000 archaeological sites in England, including barrows, camps, Roman villas and deserted villages. While some are clearly visible, many lie hidden in the ground. All are of interest because of the information they hold about past communities.

In 1994, in association with the Royal Commission on the Historical Monuments of England, English Heritage commissioned Bournemouth University to undertake the first ever national census of the condition and survival of archaeological sites in England. Using a combination of field sampling and aerial photography, the *Monuments at Risk Survey* aims to quantify monuments, ancient landscapes and historic urban areas, and report on broad patterns of change, in order to inform our conservation efforts. The first reports are expected to be available in the spring of 1997, and will provide high quality, factual information to assist strategic planning and development control.

Royal Commission on the Historical Monuments of England

The Lakedown Bronze Age Barrow Group, Wiltshire

"The Character of England - Its Landscape, Wildlife and Natural Features"

In order to inform our efforts to conserve and enhance the countryside, the Countryside Commission and English Nature, with the help of English Heritage, are working jointly to prepare a Character Map, which will reflect the distinctive features of the English countryside. The revised draft of Planning Policy Guidance note 7 (PPG7), issued in July 1996, encourages local planning authorities to take the character approach into account in formulating development plans, policies and proposals, looking to use it not as an additional layer of countryside protection, but as a guide to the distinctive character of the land and the built environment, which development should respect or enhance. **The joint Map will be published in December 1996. English Nature's work on Natural Area profiles and the Countryside Commission's landscape descriptions, which will add further detail to the Map, will be published in the first half of 1997.**

BIODIVERSITY

A key objective of the United Kingdom's Biodiversity Action Plan, drawn up after the Earth Summit in Rio in 1992, is to conserve and where possible enhance wild species and wildlife habitats.

The Biodiversity Steering Group, with members from a range of representative organisations, was invited to prepare proposals for improving the conservation of our most threatened species and habitats. These would form the basis of our nature conservation effort over the next two decades. Their report *Meeting the Rio Challenge*, was published in December 1995, and includes:

● targets and action plans for 116 of our most threatened and declining species and 14 key habitats;

● proposals to improve the quality and accessibility of data and biological recording;

● proposals to increase public awareness and involvement in conserving biodiversity; and

● guidance in preparing local biodiversity plans.

The Government endorsed the main proposals of the report in its response published in May 1996[30]. We are committed to improving co-ordination at national and local levels so that progress towards the targets for key species and habitats can be monitored. In July 1996 we established a UK Biodiversity Group with members from national and local government, conservation agencies and bodies, scientific, farming and land management organisations and industry. The Group will:

● direct the implementation of the 116 species and 14 habitat action plans;

● co-ordinate the development of a national data base and local information systems;

● provide guidance on local biodiversity action plans; and

● produce a further 286 species and 24 habitat action plans by 1999.

Separate country groups and groups on national targets, information and local issues, will be established by autumn 1996.

---

[30] *The Government's Response to the UK Steering Group Report on Biodiversity, HMSO*

Dormouse Action Plan

The dormouse is one of the threatened species for which a biodiversity action plan has been prepared. In the last century, the dormouse has become extinct in up to seven counties in England, and it is now almost completely absent from the north. Even in good habitats, population density is low, at less than ten adults per hectare.

The decline is thought to be caused by changes in woodland management practice, especially the reduction in hazel coppicing, allowing livestock to graze in woodland, and developments which fragment habitats and break up natural features.

Dormouse feeding on hawthorn berry

The action plan aims to maintain and enhance dormice populations in all the counties where they still occur, and to re-establish self-sustaining populations in at least five counties where they have been lost. The work includes:

- managing woodland and hedgerows to maintain current populations and prevent future habitat fragmentation;

- identifying dormouse habitats and providing incentives to owners to manage them sensitively;

- establishing a captive breeding programme to support re-introduction;

- extending the National Dormouse Monitoring Scheme, including developing standardised survey and monitoring methods;

- developing public awareness of the dormouse as a key indicator of woodland and hedge conditions.

English Nature will launch a new Species Grant Scheme in autumn 1996 to support the Biodiversity Action Plan by making grants available for site and species management, research and monitoring, and publicity for those species for which conservation action is urgently required.

In order to improve our understanding of population trends in our wildlife, we have published a review of biological recording in the United Kingdom[31]. Further studies, on the monitoring of wildlife populations in the United Kingdom, including bats, other mammals and wild plants, were commissioned in winter 1995/96.

Farmland Birds

There is strong evidence of a marked decline in the population of many farmland birds, such as the lapwing and skylark. We are funding two research projects to try to discover more about the causes of the decline. One of these is based at the British Trust for Ornithology and aims to analyse the Common Bird Census data and some newly collected data for 19 species of farmland birds and compare these with data on changes in agricultural practice. The second is based at the University of Oxford and aims to study in detail the fluctuations in bird populations and try to relate these to particular aspects of breeding success and survival.

Adult barn owl with chicks

---

[31]*Co-ordinating Commission for Biological Recording (1995) Biological Recording in the United Kingdom: Present Practice and Future Development, DOE*

We have also taken a number of practical steps to assist farmers to manage their land in a way which helps stem the decline. MAFF funded the Royal Society for the Protection of Birds (RSPB) to produce a video and guidelines on farmland birds and in spring 1996 sent the guidelines to all larger arable farmers free of charge. MAFF has also jointly funded the stone curlew and cirl bunting recovery projects undertaken by English Nature and the RSPB.

MAFF has also introduced national management rules for set-aside which give farmers the flexibility to create diverse habitats for wildlife conservation. Research by the RSPB and other bodies shows that set-aside supports up to 15 times more farmland birds than neighbouring cropped land. Further changes to the rules on the cutting and cultivation of set-aside land, designed to benefit ground nesting birds, were announced in April 1996.

AGRICULTURE

The Common Agricultural Policy

Rural England set out our policies for the future of agriculture, the core of which is a fundamental reform of the Common Agricultural Policy (CAP). We support the principle of a competitive agriculture industry where relative efficiency, rather than price support and supply controls, determine production patterns. This requires CAP reforms which would progressively reduce production-related support, enabling the eventual abolition of supply controls. Any payments to compensate farmers for reductions in support or to help them adjust to the new policy environment would not be production linked and would be degressive and time-limited.

CAP reform along these lines could have both positive and negative environmental impacts. Environmental benefits would include reduced inputs and reduced incentives to crop marginal land or to overgraze land. However, it could also lead to problems such as undergrazing or abandonment of land in some areas. The net effect of any reforms is uncertain at this stage. Work to assess the environmental effects of the 1992 CAP reforms was published by the European Commission in September 1996. **The countryside agencies also aim to complete a study by the end of 1996.** A joint working party of agriculture and environment experts in the OECD is undertaking a programme of work on the environmental impact of agriculture and the effects of policy reform. This work will inform meetings of Ministers from OECD countries during 1997/98. These three pieces of work may help us to identify the types of incentives that will be needed to protect and enhance the environment and will offer a cost effective use of resources.

In the future it will be necessary for our policies to take account of potential negative environmental effects of CAP reform and the need to continue to encourage positive steps, for example, in pursuance of biodiversity action plans. On this basis, *Rural England* concluded that it is probable that there will be a continuing and perhaps increasing need for incentive schemes with specific environmental objectives. We would like to see a part of the savings from the reductions in production-oriented support made available for this purpose. **We will continue to make every effort to ensure that care for the environment is central to the development of the CAP in the years to come.** We agree with the Environment Select Committee, who in their report of April 1996 said that some of the resources freed through the liberalisation of the CAP should be retargeted to address rural social and economic needs as well as environmental objectives.

In November 1995, the European Commission tabled *Agricultural Strategy*, a paper for presentation to the Madrid European Council. This identified the need for further CAP reform to respond to the challenges posed by renewal of World Trade Organisation negotiations on agriculture in 1999 and enlargement of the European Union to include the countries of Central and Eastern Europe. The European Council called for this work to be continued and further reports to be prepared. **The Commission has also undertaken to promote a debate early in 1997 on the future of the dairy regime and is committed to come forward urgently with proposals to reform the beef regime.** These initiatives provide important opportunities for reforms which reflect the priorities outlined above.

In order to provide an opportunity for new ideas to be fed into policy making and to help increase the weight given to environmental considerations, we have asked the Agriculture Commissioner to strengthen environmental and consumer representation on the European Commission's agricultural advisory committees. We hope the Commission will consider our suggestion as part of a forthcoming review of their advisory committees.

Pending reforms to the CAP, there is a need to ensure that production related payments do not in themselves encourage damaging practices and to look for ways of extending cross-compliance wherever it is practicable and sensible to do so. In July 1996 MAFF produced guidance which explains the purpose and nature of the existing cross-compliance provisions of headage payment schemes and how we implement them. *Your livestock and your landscape*, which was issued to all farmers claiming livestock subsidies, explains how to recognise and avoid the environmental damage that can be caused through overgrazing and unsuitable supplementary feeding practices. In July 1996, the Agriculture Council extended cross-compliance to the fruit and vegetable sector: new operational programmes funded by the European Union must include action to develop the use of environmentally sound cultivation and waste management techniques.

An independent study[32] examining the scope for wider application of cross-compliance in the CAP was published in November 1995, and has been widely disseminated. We would like the report to stimulate an informed and constructive debate across Europe.

Indicators of Environmental Pressures from Agriculture

Sound policies for the countryside and the wider environment need to be based on the best available information on the pressures arising from agriculture and other significant activities. Indicators are quantified information which help to explain how trends are changing over time.

MAFF has begun work to provide measures of some of the pressures which agriculture exerts on the environment and to enable changes in the scale of these pressures to be monitored. These indicators will help us to identify priorities for action or new policy directions in relation to the most significant environmental pressures from agriculture. The lessons learned should also help determine whether environmental targets are a suitable tool to carry forward policy objectives in any of these areas.

The *Indicators of Sustainable Development Report*[33] (described in Chapter One) already contains a number of indicators relevant to agriculture. However, in most cases, although these indicators track environmental changes, they do not identify the extent and nature of agriculture's contribution.

[32]*Cross-Compliance within the Common Agricultural Policy: a Review of the Options for Landscape and Nature Conservation, Institute for European Environmental Policy*
[33]*Indicators of Sustainable Development in the United Kingdom, HMSO, March 1996*

We are currently developing indicators of pesticide use, emissions of ammonia and greenhouse gases, and nutrient losses to water. We are also considering soil indicators in the context of the Government response to the Royal Commission on Environmental Pollution report on the sustainable use of soil. In addition, we are playing an active part in an OECD initiative to develop a set of agri-environment indicators.

Pesticides play an essential part in modern agriculture but, if not used responsibly, they can be harmful to man and the environment. There are difficulties in constructing an indicator which adequately reflects environmental impact as there are several hundred different pesticide ingredients with different effects; their use will vary with changes in weather and pest incidence as well as crops grown; and potential environmental damage may depend as much on the timing and method of application as on the volume and toxicity of the pesticides used. We are considering whether the construction of an index of environmental risk for each of the main pesticide groups (fungicides, insecticides etc.) through the combination of data on usage and toxicity would resolve these difficulties. **We hope that this work will provide a basis for tracking the environmental impact of pesticide use over time and that initial results may be available in 1997.**

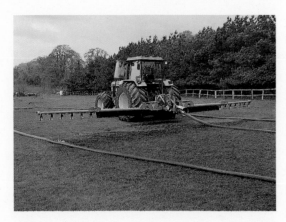

Ammonia is emitted from livestock manures. It can have a damaging environmental effect when deposited on sensitive ecosystems, through acidification and eutrophication[34], although it also provides potentially beneficial nutrients if deposited on agricultural land. A national inventory of ammonia emissions is calculated for agriculture, but current estimates contain a large margin of error. Improvements are needed in the accuracy of estimated emissions for each type of animal and management system and in information on the proportion of farms using each type of system. **We aim to provide an improved estimate of these agricultural emissions by June 1997 based on new survey data.**

Correct timing and application methods for spreading livestock slurry can maximise the benefit to the crop and reduce losses to the environment.

Agriculture is a significant source of methane and nitrous oxide which contribute to the greenhouse effect. An assessment of agriculture's contribution to total emissions of these gases can only be made through modelling, since total emissions cannot be measured at source. Current estimates, which form part of the UK national inventory of greenhouse gas emissions, are very provisional. In order to improve them, we need a better understanding of how farming methods, such as fertiliser practice and animal diets, affect emissions, and better data on the prevalence of different farm practices. **We have work in hand in both these areas and will continuously refine the estimates. We would hope, as results become available, to achieve major improvements by 1999 or soon after.**

Nitrates can cause water pollution in some areas, and the main source of nitrate in water is agriculture. A key project within MAFF's £5.4 million annual programme on nitrate losses from agriculture will develop a modelling framework which will allow the estimation of nitrate losses at the regional and river catchment level. There is some way still to go in this work. First the necessary data and modelling techniques must be brought together. Then we will need to resolve issues such as how catchment by catchment estimates should be aggregated to produce a national indicator and whether distinctions should be made between losses to surface water (where the environmental effect is fairly direct) and losses to groundwater (where effects are normally delayed, gradual and cumulative). **We aim to provide initial catchment models by 1998, and a national indicator in 1999.**

---

[34] *Nutrient enrichment of water or land which accelerates the growth of less desirable species.*

Phosphorus can be a source of water pollution: the prime source in rivers is domestic sewage, though about 20% comes from agriculture. MAFF work to develop a national model of phosphorus loss from agriculture is at a very early stage, mainly due to inadequacy of data on the relationships between soil type, weather and farm practices and the different forms of loss such as soil erosion, leaching and manure run-off. **Drawing on research results as they become available, we aim to provide a national indicator of losses in 1999.**

AGRI-ENVIRONMENT SCHEMES

Our incentive schemes encourage farmers and others to provide environmental benefits beyond the legal requirements placed on them. Through our environmental land management schemes, we give priority to those areas and features that:

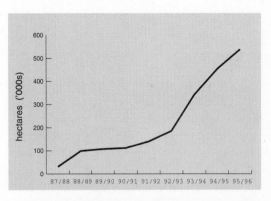

- are valuable to the countryside but are in decline or under threat;

- have significant potential to provide new environmental benefits;

- are in need of positive management to maintain and enhance their value.

Land subject to agri-environment agreements

Around 6% of our agricultural area is now subject to an agri-environmental agreement, with a total of over 13,000 separate agreements with farmers.

Agri-environment schemes will have an important role in helping to achieve the targets in the action plans drawn up by the Biodiversity Steering Group; we will seek to make the most effective use of them through national and local targeting. Countryside Stewardship is particularly well placed to help implement local biodiversity action plans because its priorities are assessed at a local level, in consultation with representatives of voluntary conservation organisations, farmers and land-owners. **Over the next five years, as the schemes are reviewed, we will invite proposals as to how they might be revised, including how they might make a strengthened contribution to the biodiversity targets.**

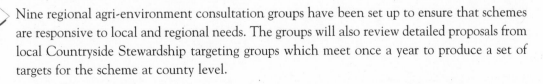

Rural England announced the creation of a national Agri-Environment Steering Group of Government Departments and agencies to keep under review the integration and focus of environmental land management schemes, together with a new National Forum for regular consultation with a wide range of interested parties, and separate regional consultation arrangements. The Steering Group met for the first time in October 1995 and will meet quarterly. The new National Forum held its first meeting in March 1996, with some 27 organisations invited to attend, including Government Departments and agencies, voluntary conservation organisations and representatives of farmers and land managers. Members of the Forum welcomed the opportunity to contribute to policy development. Among the issues discussed were regional consultation arrangements, priorities for the use of resources, the dissemination of information and encouragement of collaborative activities. A working group to look at further ways of enhancing the conservation value of arable land was set up. The next meeting of the Forum will be held in October 1996.

Nine regional agri-environment consultation groups have been set up to ensure that schemes are responsive to local and regional needs. The groups will also review detailed proposals from local Countryside Stewardship targeting groups which meet once a year to produce a set of targets for the scheme at county level.

Environmentally Sensitive Areas (ESAs)

The ESA scheme provides ten year management agreements to conserve 22 nationally important areas. 10% of the agricultural land in England is eligible under the scheme, and take up covers 44% of the eligible area. Objectives are set for each ESA, under the broad aim of maintaining and enhancing the landscape, wildlife and historic value of the land by encouraging beneficial farming practices.

Under a cyclical five year programme the environmental achievements of the five earliest ESAs to be created have been evaluated: **MAFF will publish the results in autumn 1996.** The main aim of the ESAs was to reverse the rapid deterioration of the landscape and wildlife of the areas; the evaluation showed a positive outcome in that:

● intensification of agriculture in the Somerset Levels and Moors, West Penwith and the Pennine Dales had largely been halted;

● in the Broads and South Downs ESAs the quality of the landscape has been considerably enhanced by the reversion of arable land to grassland;

● the wildlife conservation interest on ESA land, both flora and fauna, has been protected and increased; for example there are greater numbers of wading birds in the Somerset Levels and more plant species in hay meadows in the Pennine Dales.

MAFF

Following consultation with farming and conservation bodies, we have issued proposals for improvements to these five ESA schemes for the next five years. The proposed changes to the schemes have been designed to strengthen their role in increasing biodiversity. **Current monitoring of eleven more ESAs will be evaluated and the schemes reviewed in 1997.**

We also look for opportunities to introduce changes between five year reviews: for example, in June 1996 we added grants for the creation and restoration of ponds to some ESAs.

Pennine Dales - hillside meadow

Countryside Stewardship

Rural England gave high priority to Countryside Stewardship, as our main environmental incentive scheme for the wider countryside outside ESAs. The scheme provides ten year management agreements for conserving and improving the beauty of the landscape, wildlife habitats, historic features and providing better access to the countryside. By March 1996, over 90,000 hectares of land were in the scheme, which had achieved a high degree of success in meeting its environmental objectives. For example, over 2,000 kilometres of hedge have already been restored, with another 1,600 kilometres to be completed under existing agreements.

In April 1996, the scheme was transferred to MAFF from the Countryside Commission and relaunched in an expanded form, with £5 million for new agreements in 1996 and a further £5 million for 1997. Well over 2,000 applications were received in the 1996 application period - more than double the previous year.

By encouraging the improvement of field boundaries and the margins of arable fields, which the Biodiversity Steering Group identified as a priority, the scheme now gives particular emphasis to arable areas. The need to conserve the remaining old meadows and pastures of England, another important biodiversity habitat, is also emphasised.

Countryside Restoration Trust, Cambridgeshire

The Countryside Restoration Trust has forged a creative partnership between the voluntary and public sectors in order to transform intensively farmed land into environmentally rich habitat. With the help of Countryside Stewardship, the Trust has transformed over 18 hectares of wheat fields into a mixture of arable land and grassland, planting hedgerows and creating field margins and conservation headlands. These new habitats have attracted many forms of wildlife, in particular common blue, brown argus and small copper butterflies. The brown hare and grey partridge have both shown dramatic increases.

By raising the water level in Bourn Brook, a tributary of the River Cam, the Environment Agency has helped to consolidate the return of otters. The Trust has reintroduced lost water plants such as the marsh marigold, yellow iris, water avens and flowering rush, and in 1996, for the first time in many years, kingfishers and yellow wagtails are breeding nearby.

Organic Farming

We are committed to encouraging an increase in organic farming, which has a positive and distinct role to play as part of our wider efforts to promote environmentally friendly farming and a "greener" CAP.

- We support the United Kingdom Register of Organic Food Standards (UKROFS) and the development of European Union and world standards.

- We fund around £1 million worth of dedicated research and development a year.

- The Organic Aid Scheme provides financial support for conversion to organic standards.

In order to ensure that farmers are aware of the opportunities and to help them assess whether they might profit from conversion to organic standards, MAFF launched the Organic Conversion Information Service in June 1996. The service is co-ordinated by ADAS and provides a dedicated telephone helpline and free advisory visits to farmers. The helpline, operated by the Soil Association, provides basic information on production standards, registration and the support available for conversion. Advisory visits, undertaken by a team of experts from the Elm Farm Research Centre, provide detailed technical advice on conversion and marketing, tailored to the needs of the individual holding.

Wildlife Enhancement Scheme (WES)

In April 1996, building on earlier trials, English Nature re-launched the WES as a national scheme. By providing standard payments within management agreements, this scheme encourages positive management of Sites of Special Scientific Interest (SSSIs). By June 1996, there were 339 WES agreements, covering 12,060 hectares.

Free Advice

Sound advice and encouragement remains a key method of helping farmers maintain and improve the environment. In the past year, we have funded some 3,000 free farm pollution prevention visits and 1,495 free conservation visits by ADAS. The Farming and Wildlife Advisory Group (FWAG), provided 3,835 conservation advice visits. In October 1995, FWAG launched a new, more structured advice service - *Landwise* - for which we have made available increased funding.

 A recent evaluation of the Codes of Good Agricultural Practice for Air, Soil and Water found that the content and presentation were generally well received, but that more could be done to ensure their effective distribution. **We therefore intend to revise and relaunch them in 1997.**

Pesticides

Our policy is to limit pesticide use to the minimum necessary for the effective control of pests and diseases, subject to overriding considerations of human health and environmental impact.

 In October 1995, we held a conference to bring together the views of those concerned with the use and effects of pesticides. This led to the creation, in May 1996, of the Pesticides Forum, comprising representatives from agricultural, environmental, consumer, research and training groups. The Forum will meet about three times a year. It will advise Government on the promotion and implementation of the responsible use of pesticides, as well as helping to disseminate best practice, advances in technology and R&D results. **A priority task for the Forum will be the development of an action plan for the responsible use of pesticides which will include measures for encouraging the widespread adoption of appropriate integrated crop management techniques. The action plan will be in place by the end of 1997.**

The Campaign Against Illegal Poisoning of Wildlife aims to discourage the abuse of pesticides.

In May 1996, we published a booklet *Pesticides and Integrated Farming*, which provides general advice to farmers and growers on ways in which they can minimise their use of pesticides. It encourages users to:

● use pesticides only where absolutely justified and cost effective;

● consider combining chemical and non-chemical controls;

● use the right product at the right time;

● seek expert advice if in any doubt as to what controls might be used.

> **Technologies for Sustainable Farming Systems**
>
> The LINK programme, which is jointly funded by Government and industry, supports research on lower-cost production methods which meet environmental and consumer requirements. The work points to ways of reducing inputs such as pesticides and fertilisers whilst maintaining profitability.
>
> Preliminary findings from the Integrated Farming Systems project, published in June 1996, have shown that while yields have tended to be lower than from conventional systems, profitability has often been maintained by savings on input costs and higher premia for quality. The project will run until March 1998, and further research is analysing the implications of integrated systems for labour and machinery requirements and work patterns.

Common Land

Emphasising the importance of common land for farmers, wildlife and those seeking recreation, *Rural England* endorsed the rights of commoners and the need for proper management of commons. In August 1996, we let a contract to produce a Guide to Good Practice in the Management of Common Land, drawing on the advice of a wide range of organisations representing all interests in common land. **We hope to publish the Guide in the autumn of 1997.**

FORESTRY

Woodland Expansion

Forests offer us many benefits. They provide timber and are a source of income and employment. They provide opportunities for recreation and leisure, for wildlife conservation and for enhancing the landscape. Yet only 7% of England is wooded - less than almost every other European country. *Rural England* set the long term aspirational target of doubling woodland in England over the next half century in order to stimulate fresh thinking and debate about the opportunities for woodland expansion. Implementation of this target will depend upon necessary reforms of the Common Agricultural Policy, and on action by a wide range of landowners and organisations.

The Government Panel on Sustainable Development issued its second report in January 1996 which supported the broad aim of the aspirational target and called for more work on how it could be achieved. In order to help elaborate a way forward, **the Forestry Authority and the Countryside Commission will publish a discussion document in October 1996 on opportunities for woodland expansion.**

In its report on *Rural England*, the Environment Select Committee expressed concern that a rapid increase in the rate of planting might result in a deterioration in environmental standards. Adequate safeguards are already in place to prevent this. Since 1988 all plantings under the Woodland Grant Scheme have had to comply with the Forestry Authority's detailed environmental guidelines which describe the basic standard expected in any application for grant aid, while the Environmental Assessment Regulations provide further safeguards. In June 1996 the Forestry Authority circulated a consultation document on *The UK Forestry Standard*. **We aim to publish an updated Standard which will assist in the implementation of the guidelines in different forest types by spring 1997.**

In May 1996, we announced revisions to the consultation procedures for forestry planting and felling proposals, in order to speed up grant applications, while continuing to safeguard the environment. A new public register of applications, available in local authority planning offices, and in due course, on the Internet, will give the public a greater opportunity to comment, while special arrangements will apply to consultation in sensitive areas.

Planting in England in 1995/96 was around 4,500 hectares. Of this, 240 hectares was planted in the National Forest, and 945 hectares in the Community Forests. Under the Farm Woodland Premium Scheme, planting of 2,357 hectares was approved in 1995/96.

Incentives for Forestry

The Farm Woodland Premium Scheme encourages farmers to plant woodlands by making available annual payments over a period of 10 or 15 years to help offset the agricultural income foregone. In August 1996, following a review of the scheme, we published a consultation document describing a number of proposed changes to the scheme.[35] Our proposals include:

● integrating the scheme more closely with the Woodland Grant Scheme through a joint application procedure;

● higher payment rates for plantings on arable land than for plantings on improved permanent grassland;

● abolishing the rule limiting applications to 50% of the farm area, but introducing a 200 hectare limit on total plantings per farm business; and

● removing the requirement for participants to continue to run an agricultural business.

We intend to introduce changes from 1 April 1997.

The 1994 review of forestry incentives introduced some pilot schemes to test ways of targeting planting incentives in areas of greatest priority. These were the National Forest Tender Scheme, the Locational Supplement for Community Forests and the Woodland Improvement Grant. In the first round of the National Forest Tender Scheme, 181 hectares of woodland were planted, with all sites offering access of some kind, and many providing recreation and environmental benefits of the highest quality. The results of the second round, announced in October 1996, will add a further 336 hectares. Under the Locational Supplement, 75 hectares had been planted in the 12 Community Forests up to 31 March 1996. **The operation of these pilot schemes will be reviewed in 1997, with a view to assessing whether these approaches could be extended to other areas.**

In addition to forestry grants, a wide range of other funding mechanisms can support forestry related activities. Community Forests have been especially successful in attracting grants from the European Regional Development Fund and the National Heritage Memorial Fund to plant multi-purpose woodland in urban and urban fringe areas. In spring 1996 the Mersey Forest received a £349,000 grant under the Objective 1 Programme and in December 1995, an £860,000 Objective 2 grant was awarded to the Red Rose Forest near Manchester. The Great Western Community Forest received £685,000 from the National Heritage Memorial Fund towards the restoration of the historic Stanton Park in April 1996, while in March, the Greenwood Community Forest received £75,000 from the same Fund towards environmental improvements in the Erewash Valley.

Community Forest Achievements

Community Forest Project Teams began work in 1991 in most of the twelve Forests. Some of their achievements are:

(In hectares)	1991-96	1995-96
New planting	3,440	945
Existing woodland brought into management	8,445	1,317
Woodland newly opened for recreation and access	4,408	2,300
New non-woodland habitat created or brought into management	3,885	824
Derelict land reclaimed to multi-purpose forestry uses	390	143

[35] *Farm Woodland Premium Scheme, a Consultation Document from the Agriculture Departments.*

Environmental Regeneration

Forestry techniques can make a valuable contribution to environmental regeneration and we are supporting a number of initiatives which will have wider community benefits. In January 1996 we formally launched the National Urban Forestry Unit with the remit of promoting cost effective woodland planting in urban areas, especially on derelict sites. During 1996, the Unit:

- won an £8 million Millennium Award to support 600 hectares of new planting in the Black Country;

- held seminars in the North East and in the Thames Gateway to discuss the opportunities for urban forestry to complement regeneration of the built environment in these areas; and

- started work with the National Forest to develop an Urban Forestry Strategy for Burton-upon-Trent.

The reclamation of derelict land for forestry use provides an opportunity for increasing woodland cover. The Forestry Commission and the National Urban Forestry Unit have commissioned Manchester University to investigate the scope for forestry on derelict and vacant land. The project will help in assessing where forestry can be used to best advantage. **The research will be completed by the autumn of 1996.**

The National Forest

The National Forest Company was established in April 1995 to encourage the creation of new multi-purpose woodlands in a 200 square mile area of the East Midlands. The Forest will provide many economic, environmental and amenity benefits. The Company aims to reafforest a third of the area in the long term, and 9,000 hectares by 2005. Since 1991, when a development team first started working in the Forest area, over 800 hectares and a million trees have been planted, and over 100 hectares of new habitats have been created.

The Company is successfully promoting partnerships with local authorities and others to bid for regeneration funding in the area and has secured over £12 million for forest related projects. This includes a £4.9 million Heart of the Forest centre at Moira, supported by the Rural Development Commission, English Partnerships, the European Union's RECHAR programme and others.

The National Forest Company offices at the Heart of the Forest Centre at Moira. This is a restored colliery site.

In order to attract funding from other sources, including donations from the private sector, voluntary organisations and members of the public, the Company aims to establish a charity. **We are considering detailed proposals and hope that the charity will be established by April 1997.**

In April 1996, the DOE and Forestry Authority completed a three year research project in the National Forest on planting techniques on old and newly reclaimed land. This identified the best techniques and species to use in different soil types. It also tested the opportunities for planting short rotation coppice on derelict land. The demonstration sites are always open to the public and the Company can provide guided visits. **The results of the research will be published in autumn 1996.**

Barnsley Metropolitan Borough Council

The Trans Pennine Trail is a long distance coast to coast route across northern England for walkers, cyclists and horse riders, using canal towpaths, new and existing footpaths and old railway lines. Over 400 miles of trail from Southport in the west to Hornsea in East Yorkshire, with links to Chesterfield, Leeds, Sheffield and York, were officially opened in July 1996.

RECREATION AND ACCESS

Recreation in the countryside is important both as a source of income and employment for rural communities and as a way in which urban and rural residents alike can enjoy the countryside. Our priorities are therefore to:

- promote countryside recreation because it enriches the nation as a whole;

- pursue policies which enable people to enjoy the countryside where they live;

- seek to ensure that countryside recreation takes place in ways which cause no lasting damage to the environment and respects other rural interests;

- encourage creative management of recreation in order to anticipate conflicts and resolve them at an early stage.

Ministry of Defence Land

The Defence Estate includes some of the most spectacular and important countryside in Britain, and we are committed to allowing public access where it is consistent with operational requirements and the need for safety, security and conservation.

 Walks on MOD Lands, the new edition of which was published in June 1996, provides information on a series of walks on 10 different parts of the Defence Estate. Safety has been given a higher profile in the latest edition; we have taken all reasonable precautions to ensure that the public keep to paths, that warning notices are displayed, and red flags flown whenever live firing is taking place. **We will update the booklet every couple of years, adding new areas each time if possible.**

Woodland Access

 In recognition of the recreational value of Forestry Commission woodlands, we have reviewed how access should be protected when woodlands are sold. In March 1996 the Forestry Commission published new access guidelines. Central to the new arrangements is a requirement that, in considering forests as candidates for sale, a checklist analysing public use of the forest will be completed. Local authorities will be informed of all proposed sales and will be sent a copy of the completed checklist and be able to comment on it. In all appropriate cases, the Forestry Commission will offer the local authority the opportunity to enter into an access agreement which will protect public access in perpetuity. The Forestry Commission will also be prepared to meet the reasonable legal costs of local authorities in drawing up agreements. The Government expect local authorities to give careful consideration to all such proposals, taking into account the view of local communities.

[36] *Available from Miss L Quigley, Room B4/11, Government Offices, MOD, Leatherhead Road, Chessington, Surrey.*

Farmland Access

Our agri-environment schemes provide increasing opportunities for the public to enjoy the countryside by providing payments for allowing access to farmland. Since 1991, over a thousand new access opportunities have been provided under the Countryside Stewardship, Countryside Access and Environmentally Sensitive Areas schemes. In February 1996, details of sites, including maps and features of interest, became available on the Internet.

Parish Paths and Footpaths

We wish to encourage further involvement of local people in the management of access to the countryside. We have therefore worked closely with the Countryside Commission to develop a new scheme called the Local Access Initiative which builds on the successful Parish Paths Partnership initiative. The scheme will seek to maximise the role of local people in access management and maintenance, integrate more fully the rights of way network with other access and recreational opportunities, and provide opportunities for additional access. It will also consider the relationship of local management to the accurate recording of rights of way, and look at the scope for changes to the network, including making the system for changing rights of way simpler and more flexible.

Up to four pilot projects will be established, amongst groups of parishes in varying geographic areas and reflecting a range of land uses, population densities and recreational pressures or opportunities. **We expect to announce the projects, which will be based on partnerships of local landowners, farmers, other residents and interested groups or individuals, by the end of 1996.**

Vehicles on Rights of Way

In recognition of public concerns about the damage and disturbance which the inconsiderate use of vehicles on footpaths, bridleways and open land can cause, we are reviewing the most effective ways of managing vehicles' use of rights of way.

In August 1996 we published a consultation paper[37] which proposes:

- the creation of a new class of highways with non-metalled surfaces - "byways" - on which it would no longer be legal to drive motorised vehicles except for access; and

- amendments to the Highways Acts and the Wildlife and Countryside Act 1981 to alter the classes of ways to be included on definitive maps of rights of way and the procedures for establishing where vehicular rights exist.

We will announce our future intentions by spring 1997, taking account of responses to the consultation.

In the meantime, in autumn 1996 we will publish a good practice guide on ways of managing existing use of rights of way by vehicles, containing practical advice on procedures and policies towards the management and maintenance of those rights of way where vehicular rights exist.

---

[37] *Motorised Vehicles on Byways, DOT/DOE*

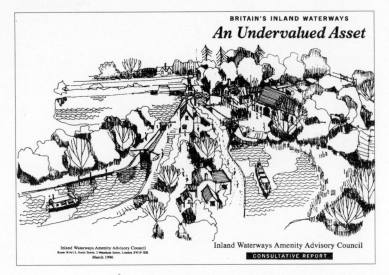

BRITAIN'S INLAND WATERWAYS
An Undervalued Asset

Inland Waterways Amenity Council
Room N14/13, North Tower, 2 Marsham Street, London SW1P 3EB
March 1996

Inland Waterways Amenity Advisory Council
CONSULTATIVE REPORT

Inland Waterways

England's waterways, which are widely used for recreational boating, angling and walking, form a valuable link between rural and urban areas. In May 1996, the Inland Waterways Amenity Advisory Committee published a consultative report - *Britain's Inland Waterways: An Undervalued Asset*, which proposes ways of enhancing the value of waterways. Following consultation, which ended on 31 August 1996, the Committee are planning a seminar in November, which will inform recommendations to Government.

 In February 1995, we consulted on the options for the future administration of Britain's waterways. We have now concluded that in view of the diversity of purpose and nature of the different waterways, administration of all of them by a single national body would not be appropriate. We have therefore invited British Waterways and the Environment Agency to review jointly the administration of certain waterways. **This work is expected to be completed before the end of 1996 and decisions on any transfer of responsibility for individual waterways to be taken in 1997.**

Meanwhile, we have invited all navigation bodies to increase their joint working on practical measures such as boat safety and streamlined licensing, and to work through voluntary co-operation with waterway users and other interests to develop a strategic approach to maximise the benefits of the waterways.

BUILT ENVIRONMENT

Rural England recognised the vulnerability of the English countryside. It emphasised the need to assess the impacts of development on the environment, and to find ways of:

- managing demand for land and other valuable resources more prudently, for example by targeting as much building as possible on land which has already been developed, rather than on green-field sites;

- designing necessary development with more imagination and sensitivity so that it reinforces local character and is acceptable to local people; and

- ensuring that natural resources are used in ways that minimise harm to the surrounding environment.

Accommodating New Housing

Projections suggest that up to 4.4 million additional households could form in the United Kingdom over the 25 years from 1991. This poses a major challenge for Government, local planning authorities, housebuilders and local communities.

The projections represent an increase in households of 23%, although urban land is projected to increase by only 12.2% because of the increased recycling of previously developed land. Even so, the projections are equivalent to a change from rural to urban uses of land of 6,800 hectares each year.

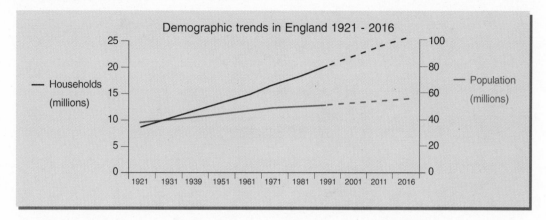

Demographic trends in England 1921 - 2016

In order to minimise the need to develop greenfield sites, we are seeking to concentrate development in urban areas and on derelict and degraded "brownfield sites". In July 1995, the Housing White Paper *Our Future Homes* set a national target of half of all new housing to be built on land which has been previously developed for urban uses by 2005. In 1985, 38% of the land developed for new housing had been previously developed. By 1993, this proportion had increased to 49%. Although the target of 50% has almost been achieved, there is some evidence that the brownfield sites which are easiest to develop are becoming more scarce, so maintaining a 50% recycling rate will remain a challenge and require greater effort in targeting vacant and previously developed sites.

The 50% target is a national average and conceals significant regional variations. There is thus considerable scope for increasing land recycling in many areas.

Percentage of land developed for new housing that was previously developed				
Government Office Regions	1990	1991	1992	1993
Eastern	46	42	46	49
East Midlands	36	33	34	32
London	79	83	84	83
Merseyside	52	48	65	76
North East	35	42	47	41
North West	46	49	54	56
South East	53	50	49	50
South West	34	30	36	33
West Midlands	39	44	47	50
Yorkshire and Humberside	38	38	43	49
ENGLAND	44	44	47	49

In autumn 1996, we will publish a discussion paper in order to stimulate public debate on how best to accommodate the rising number of households. This will explore both the origins and nature of the growth, and will assess the relative merits of alternative ways of responding to the projections.

The Government Panel on Sustainable Development is investigating the scope for increasing the target from 50% to 75%. Meanwhile we have commissioned a number of studies into ways of facilitating further urban development, including studies on density, environmental capacity, intensification and quality, which will be published during 1997.

It is important that we make the best use of the homes we have, in order to minimise the need to build new houses. A key target for the next decade is to reduce the proportion of homes lying empty to 3% of the total stock.

Number of vacant dwellings in England			
	1993	1994	1995
Total stock[1]	19,943,957	20,073,377	20,266,776
Total vacant	869,000	845,000	803,000
Vacant as % of total	4.3%	4.2%	4.0%

[1] *Of which over 75% is in the private sector.*

Design

The Urban Design Campaign, launched in June 1995, has promoted debate about how the design of streets and buildings should relate to the character of the local area, and sought to stimulate new thinking about how development can bring economic and environmental improvements. In September 1996, we commissioned a wide ranging study to review approaches to design issues within the planning process. **This study will lead to a good practice guide on design, which we will publish in 1997.**

Award schemes can help to spread awareness of good design: the Civic Trust's Special Rural Housing Award, sponsored by the Rural Development Commission, is given every other year to the best rural housing development; judges in the 1997 competition will be looking for schemes which, through the use of imaginative high quality design, appropriate materials and attention to detail, make a positive contribution to their surroundings. Both new buildings, and restoration and conversion schemes will be considered. We are currently seeking suitable

sites for a new competition to encourage sensitive design of new low cost homes in rural areas in conjunction with the Royal Institute of British Architects.

In order to develop ways of understanding and influencing the design of buildings in rural areas, the Countryside Commission has promoted the preparation of rural design summaries by local planning authorities. In autumn 1996, the Commission published two sets of detailed guidance, on the preparation of countryside design summaries and village design statements. Both were circulated to every local planning authority in England; the village design guidance was also circulated to County Associations of Local Councils and Rural Community Councils.

Design Guide for Agricultural Buildings

The North Pennines Area of Outstanding Natural Beauty (AONB) covers a wide geographical area, including parts of County Durham, Northumberland and Cumbria. The AONB designation confers on the local authorities a special responsibility to preserve and enhance the character and appearance of the area, which is characterised by small, traditionally built farmsteads and field barns. However, traditional buildings are often not suitable for the needs of modern agriculture and many farmers need to erect new buildings.

Westgate, Weardale

In order to help farmers and landowners take account of the particular sensitivities influencing agricultural development in the AONB, MAFF, in conjunction with local authorities, is preparing a design guide, which will give practical advice on the siting, design and appearance of new farm buildings and structures. The guide, which was issued in draft for consultation in July 1996, will also provide guidance to planning officers on the agricultural considerations. **We expect that the Guide will be published by the end of 1996. We will consider whether this approach could be extended to other parts of the countryside.**

Intrusive Lighting

Insensitive or excessive lighting continues to be of concern to many who live in, or visit, rural areas. In response to this concern, we invited the Countryside Commission to develop a best practice guide for lighting for rural roads. Early in 1996, this project was expanded to embrace insensitive lighting from a variety of sources, not just from roads. **The work is expected to be completed by March 1997.**

Coastal Management

The need to reconcile leisure demands, economic development and conservation presents particular challenges in the coastal zone. We have taken a number of measures to help improve management:

● in November 1995 we published *Policy Guidelines for the Coast*, which draws together current policy and guidance on a wide range of issues affecting the coast;

● we will follow this, in October 1996, with *Coastal Zone Management - Towards Best Practice* which reviews a variety of local arrangements for managing estuaries and other coastal zones; and

● as part of a review of bye-law making powers for the coast, **we expect to issue a consultation paper before the end of 1996**.

Skinningrove Beck

Action by local people is helping to improve the quality of the coastline in Cleveland. The water in Skinningrove Beck on the Cleveland coast runs orange because of rust pollution from old ironstone workings. Other problems include derelict industrial sites and eroding slopes, a lack of amenity value for local people and increasing pressure of visitors to the Heritage Coast. A local group based on the community-run Loftus Development Trust has investigated a comprehensive package of environmental improvements to the beck and its "corridor".

In May 1996, a Rural Action project grant funded a study which examined:

- water quality problems;
- the potential for improving footpaths and access;
- enhancing the area's potential for wildlife, heritage and recreation;
- the potential for tourism development; and
- ways of making local industrial sites more attractive.

During the summer, the group consulted local residents, landowners and businesses.

Loftus Town Council has provided funding towards meeting the costs of the project, while the Environment Agency is providing substantial technical help with water sampling, and Northumbrian Water is carrying out a parallel investigation into improvements in sewage outfall in the area. The initiative is expected to lead to marked improvements during the next two years.

NATURAL RESOURCES

Our countryside provides many of the natural resources on which we depend. All are limited, some are irreplaceable. They should be used with respect for the environment from which they come, and with consideration for the needs of future generations.

Minerals

A wide range of minerals is worked in England for construction, energy and other industrial purposes. Where extraction is necessary, we expect operations to meet modern environmental standards, both during and after use. In pursuit of this objective, in September 1995, we published Minerals Planning Guidance note (MPG) 14 *Review of Mineral Permissions*, which provides advice on reviewing minerals sites which were granted permission before 1982. This should lead to up-to-date planning conditions for all mineral workings.

During 1996, DOE further developed its research programme on good practices for reducing the environmental effects of mineral workings, commissioning research on the effects of particulate emissions from opencast coal workings. Work on blasting and traffic associated with quarrying will be published in autumn 1996, and a project to examine the effect of quarrying on surface and ground water was started in July 1996. We intend to revise MPG2 *Applications, Permissions and Conditions,* to take account of the results of this research, and to publish it in 1997.

In pursuit of our aim to reduce our reliance on primary aggregates, we are currently reviewing the extent to which the principle of sustainable development is being applied to extraction of aggregate minerals. **We have initiated research to evaluate how the supply of aggregates is planned and expect to publish the results in 1998.**

We also aim to encourage more use of recycled and secondary materials. MPG6 on aggregates provision therefore invited primary aggregate producers to advise on the steps that should be taken to increase the use of recycled and secondary aggregate materials. **Industry views will be reflected in the biennial report on MPG6 which we will publish by the end of 1996.** Meanwhile we are examining whether the establishment of an Aggregates Advisory Service, to provide advice and to encourage the use of reclaimed and secondary aggregates, would be an effective way to promote the increased use of alternatives to primary aggregates. **A trial of the service will be undertaken during 1997.**

Peat

The extraction of peat continues to be of concern to conservation interests. MPG13, published in July 1995, provides a new framework for securing peat supplies, whilst minimising environmental damage. In addition, we would like to see more use made of alternative materials in order to reduce the need for peat. **We have therefore commissioned a three year research programme to monitor the extent to which alternatives are being used. This will begin in the autumn of 1996 and the first report will be available towards the end of 1997.**

Soil

Soil is a limited resource, essential for the production of our food and other products, and as an ecosystem for vital organisms. Our overall objective is to protect land as a natural resource and an important part of this is the conservation of soil. We therefore welcome the report which the Royal Commission on Environmental Pollution (RCEP) published in February 1996. This examined five key policy areas:

● the deliberate removal of soil in the course of extracting peat and other minerals;

● the use of soils for farming and forestry;

● the spreading of sewage sludge and other wastes onto soil;

● the landfilling of wastes; and

● the contamination of soils from past and present industrial operations.

The report recommended that a soil protection policy should be drawn up, taking account of long-term environmental considerations. **We aim to publish a formal response to this, and the other recommendations, before the end of 1996.**

Waste

The countryside must inevitably absorb much of the waste generated by our towns and cities, as well as rural communities. In disposing of waste it is important to minimise the impact on the rural environment. The key objectives of our waste strategy are to:

- reduce the amount of waste requiring final disposal by reduction, re-use and recycling of waste;

- ensure an adequate supply of waste management facilities are available;

- encourage working practices, which preserve and enhance the overall quality of the environment;

- protect areas of designated landscape or nature conservation from development; and

- minimise the environmental impact arising from the transport of waste.

These objectives are reflected in a new Planning Policy Guidance note on Waste, which we issued in draft for consultation in June 1996. **A final version will be published by the end of the year.**

Borowash Mill - a small scale hydro scheme in the Peak District

Energy Technology Support Unit

Energy

We are continuing to encourage the provision of energy from renewable sources, such as small hydro-electric schemes, biomass, landfill and sewage gas and waste. Under the Non-Fossil Fuel Obligation (NFFO) scheme, electricity suppliers are paid premium rates by the Regional Electricity Companies. At the end of March 1996, 151 schemes were operating, many of them in rural areas.

Water Resources

Water is an essential resource for industry, power generation and irrigation, as well as drinking and washing. Recent periods of hot weather and low rainfall have reminded us of the need to use water sustainably.

In September 1995, we initiated a review of long term water supply, in conjunction with the Environment Agency, the Office of Water Services (OFWAT) and the water companies. As part of this review, data on water supply is being reassessed to take account of climate change and the effects of different patterns of vegetation such as the expansion of woodlands. Recent work by OFWAT[38], which highlighted wide variations in the quality of information on demand for water from different companies, will also be taken into account. **In autumn 1996, we will publish a report identifying the issues on which further work is needed and a timetable for completing it.**

[38]*Report on Recent Patterns of Demand for Water in England and Wales, OFWAT, May 1996*

OFWAT estimates[39] that 30% of water put into the distribution system is lost through leakage. OFWAT has also found that within companies there can be a lack of knowledge as to the most cost effective means of reducing leakage. **OFWAT will continue to monitor and report on progress in meeting leakage targets. If companies fail to set reasonable objectives or fail to deliver them, the Director General will intervene.** The Director General has also indicated that he expects water companies to analyse properly the relative costs, including to the environment, of demand management, leakage control and new investment.

Water Quality

We are taking action to improve surface water quality. The Environment Agency is considering responses to the draft proposals for statutory water quality objectives published in March 1996 **and will make formal proposals by the end of the year.** Some 90% of rivers in England and Wales are of good or fair quality and monitoring shows that in England and Wales between 1990 and 1995 there was a net improvement in class by river length of 28%.

Fisheries staff of the Environment Agency trying out a traditional rural method of gravel raking to improve salmon spawning grounds on the River Test, Hampshire.

Air Quality

Air pollution is perceived to be primarily an urban problem, but it can have significant impacts in rural areas. Some pollutants, such as ground-level ozone and sulphur dioxide, can cause direct damage to plant life, affecting both natural ecosystems and crops. Air pollution can contribute - and may in some cases be the main contributor - to other damaging processes such as acidification and eutrophication. There are likely to be effects on health and general amenity as well - ozone is the primary constituent of "summer smog", and can exacerbate respiratory problems. In particular, levels of ozone are often at their highest in rural areas, as it is formed by the action of sunlight on oxygen in the presence of chemicals which may have drifted hundreds of miles from their source.

We are addressing these issues on a number of fronts. The National Air Quality Strategy[40], launched in August 1996 contains targets for the key air pollutants which we intend to achieve by 2005. The targets, including targets for ozone and sulphur dioxide, are ambitious, and are based on standards which offer a very high level of protection to human health.

---

[39]*Leakage of Water in England and Wales, OFWAT, May 1996*
[40]*The United Kingdom National Air Quality Strategy, DOE*

5. CONCLUSION

Rural England set out to show that the countryside is properly the concern of all Departments of Government, of principal local authorities and of parish councils, of businesses and voluntary organisations, of communities and of all of us individually. It established principles to guide our approach to the countryside and an agenda for future action.

This Progress Report has endeavoured to show, one year on, how we in Government have responded to the challenge which *Rural England* posed. But this report cannot presume to be the last word. The countryside still has its share of distinctive problems as well as opportunities. There remains more for us, and for our many partners, to do in 1997 - to publish revised planning guidance for the countryside, to relieve the rateable burden on village shops, to encourage more active local citizenship and local representation by parish councils, to work towards a more equitable provision of services, to counter the ill effects of BSE. This Progress Report is part of a continuing process; we shall report again in 1997.

Luppitt Inn, Blackdown Hills

Longdendale trail

Desford Lakes, Leicestershire

Groundwork school project in Cornwall

Lydney Dial-a-Ride, Forest of Dean

Rural England's commitments are listed here in summary form. Two page numbers are provided. The number on the left refers to the original commitment made in *Rural England*. A report of progress can be found in *Rural England 1996* by reference to the page number on the right.

Printed and Published for the Controller of Her Majesty's Stationery Office
by The Stationery Office Limited
Dd 5065151, 10/96. C80, 39462, 22–0158.